THE SACRAMENTS IN PROTESTANT PRACTICE AND FAITH

James F. White

ABINGDON PRESS
Nashville

THE SACRAMENTS IN PROTESTANT PRACTICE AND FAITH

Copyright © 1999 by Abingdon Press

This book is printed on recycled, acid-free, elemental-chlorine–free paper.

Library of Congress Cataloging-in-Publication Data

White, James F.
   The sacraments in Protestant practice and faith   /   James F. White.
      p.   cm.
   Includes bibliographical references and index.
   ISBN 0-687-03402-7 (alk. paper)
   1. Sacraments.   2. Protestant churches—Doctrines.   I. Title.
BV800.W484   1999
234′.16′0882044—dc21   99-15045
                                                                                                                        CIP

Scripture quotations, unless otherwise indicated, are from the New Revised Standard Version Bible, copyright © 1989, by the Division of Christian Education of the National Council of the Churches of Christ in the United States of America.

Quotations from *The United Methodist Book of Worship* are copyright © 1992 by The United Methodist Publishing House.

03 04 05 06 07 08—10 9 8 7 6 5 4 3

MANUFACTURED IN THE UNITED STATES OF AMERICA

For

my beloved

Roman Catholic

wife,

CLAIRE DUGGAN WHITE

CONTENTS

There is a very thin line between courage and foolhardiness. To attempt to describe the sacraments in traditions as rich and varied as those within Protestantism over the course of nearly five centuries may seem to be closer to foolhardiness than courage, yet the benefits of being so bold may more than compensate. Sometimes it is helpful to see the whole forest rather than the individual trees, because recent convergences only make sense in the light of past divergences. This gives me the courage to try to take a long-range perspective so one can see how the individual components of sacramental life fit together. There are plenty of studies on the individual pieces; I am trying to put the whole puzzle together.

Ours is a time when enormous changes in sacramental life, both Protestant and Roman Catholic, are underway. Thousands of Protestant congregations have moved to a much richer and deeper observance of the sacraments in recent decades. Where the eucharist was once infrequent, it has now often become monthly or weekly. The making of new Christians through baptism has been taken much more seriously, as the new prominence of baptismal fonts or pools indicates.

At the same time, contrary movements are evident, particularly in the efforts of the church-growth movement to reach out to new or returning Christians. These churches may frequently see the sacraments as a handicap to reaching the unchurched. Some relegate the eucharist to the margins of church life and even practice rebaptism.

For Roman Catholics, nothing is stationary either. The shortage of priests increasingly makes the mass unavailable in small and remote parishes. Polls show major discrepancies between official dogma and popular belief, especially among the young. Devotions have changed even faster than the liturgy.

Evidently nothing is nailed down permanently. But it is helpful to have some perspectives to evaluate contemporary changes. That is the purpose of this book. In order to understand the present, we must have some knowledge of the past five centuries. Our survey of the past will be rapid and will always point to present realities. The European and North American backgrounds of most of Protestantism can help illumine the recent experiences of younger churches in Africa, Asia, and South America. Even the churches of Australia, New Zealand, and the Pacific islands are barely two hundred years old. So we write from a background of a limited geography to one now global.

A strong conviction of mine is that practice often shapes reflection. Thus I have put first the discussion of what the churches do and second the meanings that people derive from those practices they find familiar. Practice sometimes erupts into controversy, so I have chronicled disputes alongside the practices which sometimes provoked them. The dominant meanings at different times and churches are reviewed as a sequel to practice. There often has been a reciprocal relationship between practice and meaning. I believe one cannot dissociate what the church does from what it says it means. Liturgy and theology are intimately connected and shape each other.

Throughout, I have tried to let authors and texts speak for themselves, albeit sometimes through the translations of others or myself. This seems preferable to paraphrases, which miss the flavor and passion of what is being said. I have had to confine myself to the most important writers and texts. One could write many volumes on the Protestant sacraments if trying to reflect the contributions of the second-string varsity teams. No, I have had to limit myself only to star players.

In all cases, I have given priority to actual liturgical texts which real people have read and heard. The writings of theological mentors may have been read by thousands; the liturgies shaped the lives of millions. The United Methodist liturgies have been published in over four million hymnals; any theologian would be ecstatic to have in print one percent as many books. Liturgical texts reflect both the creative efforts of individuals in the past and the consensus of committees in the present, so they are a good index of both practices and meanings.

In dealing with the present, I have had, again, to be selective. I have chosen my examples from the four most widely used service books in American Protestantism. I believe they are representative of other service books in use in North America and much of Europe. Their similarities are more striking than their differences, yet each has distinctive characteristics. The four blend together in my mind as "MELP," i.e., United *M*ethodist Church, *E*piscopal Church, Evangelical *L*utheran Church of America, and the *P*resbyterian Church (U.S.A.). These four represent four different liturgical traditions: Methodist, Anglican, Lutheran, and Reformed. Other churches have their own books, or borrow from these four churches, or improvise their own rites.

I have tried to be impartial in describing their contents. As principal writer of the United Methodist eucharist service, I may have some prejudices but at least will reveal the intentions of the compilers of that rite, to which many others contributed.

For those who wish more background, my *Protestant Worship: Traditions in Transition* (1989) will fill in many details about the worship life of the nine Protestant liturgical traditions. Some, such as Quakers and Pentecostals, are scarcely mentioned in this book. The section "For Further Reading" lists important books on the sacraments in Protestantism beyond those listed in the notes.

One is struck by the incredibly rich and varied experiences of the various Protestant churches over the past five hundred years. This diversity has been the great contribution of Protestantism to the legacy of Christian worship. As the churches become global, it is exciting to envision the gifts the younger churches of the world will bring. My classes currently include students from Canada, Greece, Japan, Korea, Taiwan, Zimbabwe, and the Philippines. It has given my writing a new focus to realize that I am no longer addressing only citizens of the United States. I thank my students for expanding my horizons.

As I complete forty years of teaching (1959–1999), it is my fervent hope that this book will continue to teach when and where I cannot.

It is a pleasure to thank those who have contributed most directly to this book: Nancy Johnson for her careful proofreading, Cheryl Reed for deciphering my notes and typing so faithfully, and above all, my wife, Claire Duggan White, for putting up with me while I was thinking about the book and for putting up without me while I was writing it.

James F. White
University of Notre Dame

September 27, 1998

CHAPTER ONE

Sacramentality

The term *sacramentality* is relatively modern. One does not find Reformation treatises using this terminology. Yet there are a number of high-profile issues in the sixteenth century for which this modern term is appropriate. Although this may seem an anachronism, it is also helpful in showing both how much and how little has changed in nearly five centuries of Protestant sacramental life. By *sacramentality* we mean the concept that the outward and visible can convey the inward and spiritual. Physical matters and actions can become transparent vehicles of divine activity and presence. In short, sacraments can be God's love made visible.

It must be borne in mind that sacramentality is not confined to Christianity or even to religion in general. We have seen in our own time efforts to sacramentalize the American flag. For some, competitive sports take on a sacramental character. Football weekends on some college campuses have all the aura of the great holy days of the liturgical year.

Our purpose in this chapter is to describe those factors that unite the sacraments in various Protestant churches. It is natural to begin with the writings of the sixteenth-century Reformers since many of their statements still have a normative quality. But even where nuances have shifted over time, a chronological sequence seems the best way to trace these changes. Thus the sixteenth-century stratum will receive more attention than the strata laid down in subsequent centuries even though only the more recent layers may be operative today.

We begin with a brief survey of the inherited tradition of the church in the West. Then we examine some concerns about the purposes and functions of sacraments in general. This inevitably leads to the question of how many observances are to be counted as sacraments. From there we may survey how the concept of sacramentality has gradually come into its own. All this will give us background for examining the sacraments individually in subsequent chapters.

THE INHERITED SACRAMENTAL TRADITION

Most of the leaders of the sixteenth-century Protestant Reformation were priests. Both they and their flocks were deeply imbued with the sacramental life of the late medieval church of the West. For the most part, the sacramental life of the Eastern churches was not on their screen at all. It was not until the nineteenth century that reliable information about this major segment of Christianity began to be readily available and appreciated, if not appropriated. So we are dealing with the legacy of the Western half of Christianity only.

By the sixteenth century, the public worship life of Christian laity in the West was almost monopolized by the sacraments. Clergy and members of religious orders might recite the daily offices of prayer in community or, increasingly, in private. A few laypersons might own and use in private books called primers with devotional materials largely from the psalter. But these were for the literate and the affluent. The public worship of the village or city focused on the sacraments, particularly the mass.

One's entire life from cradle to grave was ministered to by the sacraments. They formed the basis of pastoral care and provided resources for each stage of life passages as well as for the day-in and day-out journey. By the late Middle Ages, birth was greeted within a very few days by baptism. Marriage was considered a sacrament, and death was preceded by a final anointing and followed by a requiem mass. In between birth and death, one might receive confirmation if a bishop chanced by and throughout life one found a remedy for sin in confession. The mass provided weekly, if not daily, encounter with Christ. Ordination was for the clergy only but they constituted a much higher percent of the population than today, in some cities 10 percent of the population.[1] The sacraments were the chief system of ministering to the people and of sustaining their religious life.

But as with all systems, there were omissions and disfunctions. The system often seemed more efficient for the work of the clergy than for the religious life of the people. The sacraments were in Latin, except for the marriage vows. What participation there was at the mass consisted largely in seeing the consecrated host, the so-called ocular communion. One sixteenth-century bishop said that "it was never meant that the people should indeed hear the Matins or hear the Mass, but be present there and pray themselves in silence."[2] Most people received communion once a year and councils had to urge them to keep even this minimum. Baptism was largely a private family ceremony, increasingly performed with a minimum of water. Confession was mandated yearly but had moved increasingly into a perfunctory juridical mode with no sense of community. Protestants were not the only critics of sacramental practice; the Council of Trent (1545–1563) called for an end to all that smacked of " 'avarice,' . . . 'irreverence' . . . [and] 'superstition' " in the mass.[3]

From the late fourteenth century onwards, a covert form of rebellion preceded the Reformation in the form of the *devotio moderna*. This was a move of piety inward, disputing the necessity, if not the efficacy, of the outward and visible sacraments. By no means a repudiation of the sacraments, it was an appeal to what seemed a more immediate reality of inward encounter with the risen Lord. Although not necessarily a precursor of the Reformation, the *devotio moderna* had many characteristics in common with movements that surfaced in the sixteenth century.

Increasingly, the sacraments had been the subject of intellectual debate. Some of this was necessitated by the proliferation of miraculous stories of bleeding hosts, kneeling donkeys, and Jews converted by the consecrated hosts. For the first eight hundred years, there had been no systematic treatise on what believers experienced in the eucharist. For nearly twelve hundred years, there had been no consensus even on how many sacraments there were. Augustine had mentioned several dozen. But this freedom had come to an end in the thirteenth century with the scholastic urge to define things. A major impetus came through what became the standard theological text-book, *The Sentences*, written about 1150 by Peter Lombard, briefly bishop of Paris. Lombard tells us that "the sacraments of the new law . . . are: baptism, confirmation, the bread of blessing, that is, the eucharist, penance, extreme unction, orders, marriage."[4] Yet as late as 1179, the Third Lateran Council mentioned "enthronement of eccle-siastical persons or the institution of priests, . . . burying the dead" as sacraments.[5]

This freedom of interpretation was ended by the later scholastics. The seven that Lombard enumerated became definitive, and the Catholic Council of Trent said no "more, or less, than seven." Lombard had said that extreme unction "is said to have been instituted by the apostles" (James 5). A momentous shift occurred in the thirteenth-century agreement that all seven were instituted by God. Thomas Aquinas tells us that "since, therefore, the power of the sacraments is from God alone, it follows that God alone can institute the sacra-ments."[6] This statement was taken with utmost seriousness by the Protestant Reformers. The freedom that had prevailed for three-fifths of church history to speak of a wide range of activities as sacraments and not have to base them on institution by God had ended in the thirteenth century. Augustine could call the ashes of Ash Wednesday a sacrament; by the thirteenth century one could not.

And the scholastics, in trying to fit all seven sacraments into a pro-crustean bed of form (words), matter (physical elements), and minister had imposed on them definitions which were not intrinsic to them. What is the matter of marriage except the conjugal act, which was rather difficult for the church to perform? And if each sacrament had to have a precise form, does that not render actions and prayers essen-tially indifferent? The way was open to a sacramental minimalism in which baptism could be valid even if performed with a medicine drop-per. The sign value of the acts and matter was basically indifferent.[7]

A more serious problem lies in the fact that abstract theology now shapes experience rather than vice versa. It may be optimistic to say that in earlier periods the experience of the divine in the sacraments had shaped reflection upon them. But the scholastics, in their rational probing into the effects of grace in each sacrament, reversed the equa-tion that praying shapes believing. Very likely this shift never hap-pened in the East, which to this day has refused to define how many sacraments there are or the precise operation of grace in them. When

Aquinas defines "the principal effect of this sacrament [extreme unction]" as "the remission of sin as to its remnants,"[8] that becomes how anointing is experienced. The experience of the sacraments by sixteenth-century Christians was thoroughly shaped by the intellectual baggage they brought to church with them. And this formed a major part of the inheritance of the Reformation from the medieval church.

THE PURPOSES OF THE SACRAMENTS

It is only in recent times that rather abstract treatises have been written on the purposes of sacraments in general. Most Protestant writers on the subject have been more concerned to correct existing practices or to encourage certain forms of piety. And no one writes hymns about sacraments in general!

At the same time, by examining proposed reforms, we can detect across the centuries various purposes coming to the forefront and motivating change. Thus we shall be looking at matters usually incidental to writers' intentions but nonetheless echoing like a recurring theme through their arguments for reform.

The most significant document in Protestant reforms of the sacramental system was Martin Luther's treatise *The Babylonian Captivity of the Church*, first published on October 6, 1520, in Latin. It had been foreshadowed by a series of three sermons on penance, baptism, and the eucharist the previous year. They are relatively mild teaching sermons. A more radical tone appears in *A Treatise on the New Testament, That Is, the Holy Mass*, written in June or early July of 1520 and published in July. Luther begins to attack various abuses such as misconceptions about the mass as sacrifice, masses for the dead, withholding the cup from the laity, and the words of institution said silently.[9] By September, when he was writing *The Babylonian Captivity*, his thought had developed even further.

The Babylonian Captivity stands as the most important single treatise shaping all Protestant sacramental life. It articulates concerns that are still intact among most Protestants. Though frequently not acknowledging the source, virtually all Protestant theologians reflect the treatise's main points. It is not surprising that it was vigorously opposed by his Catholic contemporaries. The greatest irony is that Henry VIII of England attempted to refute it by a treatise, *Assertio Septem Sacramen-*

torum, for which he and his successors were given the title "Defender of the Faith" by Pope Leo X in 1521. Obviously, no one foresaw what faith that would be for Henry and all but two or three of his successors!

The very title, *Babylonian Captivity*, is a very unsubtle reference to the captivity of the Jews in Babylon in the sixth century B.C. But Luther probably knew that Petrarch had also used it to refer to the Avignon papacy during which fourteenth-century popes had moved to France and there were two or three rival popes simultaneously. The image is that the eucharist and the whole sacramental system (save baptism) had been held in bondage to grievous errors of doctrine and practice.

Our concern here is with the positive aspects of this document. Luther did not seek to abolish any of the sacraments although he certainly sought to reform them and determine if they all deserved to be called sacraments. He even speculates whether other things such as prayer, the Word, or the cross might be sacraments since they, too, are based on divine promises.

And that word *promise* is the key to Luther's understanding of the chief purpose of sacraments. He concludes, after some equivocation about penance, that "*it has seemed proper to restrict the name of sacrament to those promises which have signs attached to them.*"[10]

Sacraments are promises connected to visible signs, and those promises are contained in scripture. They are the explicit words of Christ found only in scripture. Luther concludes that only two meet this test: baptism and the eucharist, "for only in these two do we find both the divinely instituted sign and the promise of forgiveness of sins." Penance lacks the visible sign and is "a return to baptism."[11] The promise focuses on the forgiveness of sins: in the eucharist "the word of divine promise . . . sets forth the forgiveness of sins";[12] with baptism, "the *first* thing to be considered . . . is the divine promise" of salvation through God's forgiveness.[13] The promise is essential to salvation: "For it is not possible to believe unless there is a promise, and the promise is not established unless it is believed. But where these two meet, they give a real and most certain efficacy to the sacraments."[14] Sacraments are scriptural promises to which Christ has given a visual sign.

The concept of sacrament as promise or testament remains a main feature of Luther's sacramental theology. *Word* and *promise* seem synonymous. His Small Catechism of 1529 asks with regard to baptism, "What is this Word and promise of God?" and the answer is Mark

16:16, "He who believes and is baptized will be saved."[15] This is usually paired with Matthew 28:19, the command to make disciples and baptize all nations in the name of the Trinity. Without the Word, the water is only water, but with the Word of God, "the power, effect, benefit, fruit, and purpose of Baptism is to save."[16]

The same is true of the eucharist. Like baptism, it is "both the commandment and the promise of the Lord Christ." We have from "Christ's lips" a promise attached to the commandment ("do this"). The words are " 'This is my body, given *for you*,' 'This is my blood, poured out *for you* for the forgiveness of sins.' "[17] They are the words of Christ himself, and as such, they are infallible promises.

This became the basis of official Lutheran teaching. The Latin text of the Augsburg Confession of 1530 affirms that the sacraments are "signs and testimonies of the will of God toward us," and that they demand "faith, which believes the promises that are set forth and offered."[18] This is not simply an intellectual acceptance of the reality of the promise but a deep sense of assurance that the sacrament actually conveys the promise that accompanies it. Sacraments at heart are the offer of forgiveness of sin whether given in baptism or constantly repeated in the eucharist. Thus the sacraments are not "merely . . . marks of profession among men." God acts in them.

It is characteristic of Ulrich Zwingli, the chief reformer of Zurich, that he should give a linguistic analysis of the Latin word *sacramentum*. He found it an inadequate translation of the Greek *mystérion*. Zwingli failed to grasp the salvific power of Luther's emphasis on promise. Rather, for Zwingli "a sacrament is nothing else than an initiatory ceremony or a pledging."[19] The sacraments, he concludes, are "signs or ceremonials . . . by which a man proves to the Church that he either aims to be, or is, a soldier of Christ, and which inform the whole Church rather than yourself of your faith."[20] There has been an important shift from Luther's dependence on divine promise of forgiveness to mere "marks of profession," of public information. But the sacraments do have power to "augment faith and are an aid to it."[21] The sacraments have "virtue or power" intrinsic in themselves, such as having been instituted and received by Christ, historical factuality, taking the place and name of what they signify, representation of high things, analogy between sign and signified, and as an oath of allegiance.[22] There seems to be a basically cerebral quality about most of these powers, as if the role of sacraments is primarily to communicate information, not just to the believer but to the community to which he or she belongs.

In John Calvin we get a major shift in looking at the function of sacraments. Without denying the insights of Luther and Zwingli, Calvin approaches the sacraments from a different perspective, namely, the nature of our humanity. He defines a sacrament as "an outward sign by which the Lord seals on our consciences the promises of his good will toward us in order to sustain the weakness of our faith; and we in turn attest our piety toward him in the presence of the Lord and of his angels and before men." He claims the authority of Augustine in defining a sacrament as "a visible form of an invisible grace."[23] In these definitions, there are elements of both Luther and Zwingli. But Calvin takes the discussion forward by specifying why sacraments are a necessity.

Though humans are naturally endowed with the knowledge of God, we inevitably turn away from God through superstition, perversity, and hypocrisy. Thus we are left in a state of depravity from which only Christ can save us. In our ignorance, dullness, and weakness, we need all the help we can get. But our Creator knows our needs before we do. Hence the Word is provided along with sacraments "to establish us in faith in it."[24] As Calvin describes it:

> Our merciful Lord, according to his infinite kindness, so tempers himself to our capacity that, since we are creatures who always creep on the ground, cleave to the flesh, and, do not think about or even conceive of anything spiritual, he condescends to lead us to himself even by these earthly elements, and to set before us in the flesh a mirror of spiritual blessings. . . . Now, because we have souls engrafted in bodies, he imparts spiritual things under visible ones.[25]

For Calvin, sacramentality is based on the nature of humans and our need for visual signs. Humanity is a race that needs signs, and sacraments are God's chosen means of relating to this need. Sacraments act like a transformer adapting 440 volts into household current. We are taught by the Word and confirmed by the sacraments.

At this point, Calvin introduces an important explanation: it is the Holy Spirit that "opens our hearts for the Word and sacraments to enter in."[26] Without the Spirit, sacraments are no more than sunshine on blind eyes or a voice to the deaf. The Holy Spirit makes the sacraments operative. It is the Spirit that makes sound and sight effective to our soul. Through it both Word and sacrament work together.

Another image Calvin uses is that sacraments are seals of God's promises. As signs they are effective: "God therefore truly executes whatever he promises and represents in signs."[27] Signs effect what they signify, they do not merely inform. Thus Calvin has a high doctrine of sacraments as signs. Had he a higher estimate of our human capacity, he might not regard sacraments as being so necessary, but given his view of our condition, they become essential. And in the sacraments it is Christ who gives Himself to us. In language that sounds curiously contemporary, Calvin declares "that Christ is the matter or (if you prefer) the substance of all the sacraments."[28] The sacraments, then, "offer and set forth Christ to us" and this is possible only through the Holy Spirit. Hence we must not focus on the signs themselves but on God's use of them for salvation.[29]

The Church of England defines sacraments in a single paragraph in the Articles of Religion (1563), reflecting both Zwingli and Calvin. According to Article XXV, "Sacraments ordained of Christ be not only badges or tokens of Christian men's profession, but rather they be certain sure witnesses, and effectual signs of grace, and God's good will towards us, by the which he doth work invisibly in us, and doth not only quicken, but also strengthen and confirm our Faith in him."[30] Thus they are public pledges, as per Zwingli, but also effective signs, as per Calvin and Luther. In the final version, sacraments are effective only for worthy recipients but damnable for the unworthy. Article XXIX makes it clear of the wicked that "in no wise are they partakers of Christ" in the eucharist but only receive the sign without the reality.[31]

Reflecting their Calvinistic heritage, the Kirk of Scotland, in the 1560 Scotch Confession of Faith, insisted that the sacraments "seal in their hearts the assurance of his promise, and of that most blessed conjunction, union and society, which the elect have with their head *Christ Jesus.*" But in an unusually strong statement beyond Zwinglianism, it insists "we utterly damn the vanity of they that affirm Sacraments to be nothing else but naked and bare signs." Then it goes on in true Calvinistic fashion to insist that in baptism we are "ingrafted in *Christ Jesus*" and our sins remitted, and in the eucharist "*Christ Jesus* is so joined with us, that he becomes very nourishment and food of our souls."[32] Sacraments are thus seen as effecting what they signify, not merely representing it.

But it fell to the seventeenth-century Quakers (Society of Friends) to articulate the most radical position on the sacraments. For them, worship was "offered in the inward and immediate moving and drawing of his [God's] own Spirit."[33] Therefore, outward and visible forms were not desirable but distractions from true worship. Public assembly was essential, even "the seeing of the faces one of another" so that the individual "partakes not only of the light and life raised in himself, but in all the rest."[34]

The English Puritans insisted on the importance of sacraments as marking the "visible difference between those that belong unto the Church and the rest of the world." The grace of the sacraments is contingent "upon the work of the Spirit, and the word of institution" for worthy recipients. "The sign and the thing signified" are so mutually interdependent as to be inseparable. The signs are effective. In these brief statements of the "Westminster Confession of Faith" of 1647 there are hints of Zwingli, Calvin, and Luther combined. Most important, sacraments are efficacious signs, the sign and the reality are conjoined. As in Calvin, the sacraments of the Old Testament were also effective signs of the "spiritual things thereby signified and exhibited."[35]

All of this was utter nonsense to the Enlightenment of the eighteenth century. The belief that material objects and actions had any supernatural power of themselves was repugnant to religion based on reason alone. Immanuel Kant, the leading Protestant philosopher of this period, found any attempt to speak of means of grace in the sacraments a dangerous illusion. There might be moral values in baptism and the eucharist, but to conceive of either as a *"means of grace*—this is religious illusion which can do naught but work counter to the spirit of religion."[36] Faith in miracles, mysteries, and sacramental means of grace is simply a fanatical deceit.

For better or for worse, a large segment of Protestantism has remained in the orbit of the Enlightenment in its sacramental life. Strong suspicion remains with regard to the union of the physical and spiritual. The language of symbolism prevails in a narrow way it never did in Zwingli or the other reformers. Sacraments are seen largely in a moralistic framework, reminding us of the past work of Christ but rarely seen as a present encounter with him today. (Ironically, many who reject any sense of the sacraments as effective signs are at present insisting on a constitutional amendment to protect the American flag from desecration—other than commercialism.) Thus the eucharist has largely a Garden-of-Gethsemane piety: "could you not at least stay awake, that is, behave better?" One English bishop went so far as to speak of Christ as really absent in the eucharist since he was being remembered.

This was not the strain of John Wesley and the early Methodists. In a countercultural mode, they found the sacraments gracious forms of encounter with Christ. The sacraments were among the appointed means of grace. Baptism of infants brought regeneration; the eucharist was often discovered to be a "converting ordinance" for those whose faith had lagged. For early American Methodists, the eucharist was the climax of quarterly meetings in which the faithful rejoiced in the presence of the King in the camp.[37] But through a long process in the nineteenth century, this sacramental edge was gradually lost in Methodism, and Enlightenment ideas prevailed instead of John Wesley's rich sacramental life.

Until relatively recently, much of American Protestantism has been pervaded by a sacramental orientation that owes more to the Enlightenment than to the Reformation. Sacramental practice has for many Protestants become a marginal part of their religious life. If sacraments are seen only as portraying and not as effecting what they represent, this is probably an inevitable development. But it is not the position of most of the sixteenth-century reformers or of John Wesley. And recent polls have shown that today many younger Roman Catholics also have an Enlightenment perspective on the sacraments despite their church's teaching.[38]

THE NUMBER OF SACRAMENTS

Inevitably the question arises of how many sacraments there are. This would seem easily answered, namely two, but the story is more complex than that. And it is still far from being completely resolved even today.

As we have already seen, the question of the number of sacraments was a late arrival, the number seven not being dogmatically defined until the fifteenth century. It was reaffirmed for Catholics by the Council of Trent in 1547.

Luther's questioning of the seven first appears in the *Babylonian Captivity*. Indeed, he seems to have been making up his mind as he wrote the treatise in late September of 1520. After discussing in detail the eucharist and baptism, he begins a discussion of "the sacrament of penance." Though describing numerous abuses, he affirms that concerning "the current practice of private confession, I am heartily in favor of it."[39] There is no question of scriptural warrant for public confession; there is in particular Matthew 18:15-18, which prescribes treatment of the erring believer. Luther concludes this section "*concerning the three sacraments,*" but when he then launches into a discussion of confirmation, he instantly questions that it is a sacrament and challenges the belief that such a description of this observance and others "can be proved from the Scriptures."[40] Marriage is "regarded as a sacrament without the least warrant of Scripture."[41] In the case of ordination, "it is ridiculous to put forth as a sacrament of God something that cannot be proved to have been instituted by God" in the absence of a "single word said about it in the whole New Testament."[42] As for extreme unction, the argument that it was instituted by the apostle James fails because "no apostle has the right on his own authority to institute a sacrament, that is, to give a divine promise with a sign attached. For this belongs to Christ alone."[43] The definition of a sacrament that has emerged is that it includes both promise and sign. In the fourth from the last paragraph of the treatise, Luther finally concludes that "*there are, strictly speaking, but two sacraments in the church of God—baptism and the bread.*" Penance lacks the visible sign and is "nothing but a way and a return to baptism."[44]

This does not mean any of the seven are necessarily abandoned. The Large Catechism of 1529 speaks of "our two sacraments, instituted by Christ."[45] But penance is strenuously promoted in both catechisms. In a triptych painted by Luther's friend, Lucas Cranach the elder, in 1547, the year after Luther's death, baptism appears on the left with Philipp Melanchthon (a layman) baptizing, the eucharist as the Last Supper with Luther in disguise in the center panel, and penance on the right panel with Johannes Bugenhagen (Luther's confessor) holding the two keys. Thus penance lurks as the third sacrament.[46] The Augsburg Confession of 1530 insists that "Confession has not been abolished in our churches."[47]

In insisting on both institution by Christ and a visible sign, Luther is simply trapped by the thirteenth-century qualification that only God can institute sacraments. And that means for him a New Testament proof text, the so-called dominical injunction. Had the earlier freedom prevailed, with sacraments being instituted by apostles or subsequently (Ash Wednesday ashes, for example), Luther would not have felt compelled to restrict the number to two. Had he appealed to the freedom of an earlier age than the scholastics', there would have been no problem. But we are shaped by those who immediately precede us, and Luther followed the scholastics in demanding divine institution.

Actually, Luther was conservative by some standards. More radical reformers, the so-called Spiritual reformers, argued that rather than two, the number of outward sacraments should be zero. One of the leading spiritualists was Casper Schwenckfeld, a nobleman and lay theologian, just the type Luther had appealed to in *To the Christian Nobility of the German Nation* in 1520. But Schwenckfeld went far beyond what Luther wanted and ceased receiving communion after 1526. Schwenckfeld's approach was mystical, on the basis that "there is no other eating than the one spiritual eating and drinking of the body and blood of Christ which is done by faith."[48] He was particularly outraged by Luther's assertion that even the wicked "eats the body of Christ physically." Other Spiritualists, such as Melchior Hofmann and Sebastian Franck, also found outward forms dispensable.

The mainline reformers followed Luther closely in insisting on explicit scriptural warrant for sacraments. Calvin had a high view of the sacraments of the Old Testament (circumcision, purifications, sacrifices), but held that with the coming of Christ "two sacraments were instituted which the Christian church now uses, Baptism and the Lord's Supper." These are sacraments "for the use of the whole church." However, he does say "I would not go against calling the laying on of hands, by which ministers of the church are initiated into their office, a sacrament, but I do not include it among the ordinary sacraments."[49] Elsewhere he says, "I have not put it as number three among the sacraments because it is not ordinary or common with all believers, but is a special rite for a particular office."[50] Obviously another criterion is functioning here: commonality among all Christians.

Chapter 19 of book 4 of the *Institutes* is devoted entirely to explaining why Calvin considered only two sacraments genuine. He insists "that the decision to establish a sacrament rests with God alone. . . . The Word of God must precede, to make a sacrament a sacrament, as Augustine very well states."[51] Failing that, Calvin makes quick work of

25

demolishing the other five "counterfeit" sacraments. Penance, for example, has no "outward ceremony instituted by the Lord to confirm our faith."[52] Extreme unction is "merely playacting, by which, without reason and without benefit, they wish to resemble the apostles."[53] Anointing is not "a ceremony instituted by God, nor has it any promise."[54]

Almost all Protestants for three centuries accepted the dogma of two sacraments. A rare exception was the Moravian bishop Count Nikolaus von Zinzendorf in the eighteenth century. He argued that marriage ought to be considered a sacrament, too.

The Church of England found a convenient equivocation by declaring that "there are two Sacraments ordained of Christ our Lord in the Gospel, that is to say, Baptism, and the Supper of the Lord" but went on to say that "those five commonly called Sacraments, that is to say, Confirmation, Penance, Orders, Matrimony, and extreme Unction, are not to be counted for Sacraments of the Gospel . . . [they] have not like nature of Sacraments with Baptism, and the Lord's Supper, for that they have not any visible sign or ceremony ordained of God."[55]

This sufficed until the nineteenth century, when the Catholic Revival in the Church of England began to insist on designating all seven as sacraments. This led to considerable controversy.

Denying that a rite or ceremony is a sacrament does not mean necessarily abolishing it. Many were retained for their spiritual efficacy. One could argue, for example, that the form of confirmation in the 1549 *Book of Common Prayer* with the signing of the cross sounds like a sacrament; the rite in the 1552 edition sounds more like an ordinary blessing. Most Protestant churches have continued ordination. Luther compiled his own rite in 1539. He also prepared forms for private confession to a pastor in 1529 and 1531. All groups continued marriage. The Puritans, while denying both that marriage was a sacrament and that it was limited to Christians, judged "it expedient, that Marriage be solemnized by a lawful Minister of the Word, that he may accordingly counsel them, and pray for a blessing upon them."[56] The blessing was outlined and the vows explicitly prescribed.

Confirmation tended to disappear among most Protestants, except Anglicans, among whom it was given a great boost by King James I (reigned 1603–1625). Various forms of penance survived, as in the Puritan days of public fasting and humiliation. Extreme unction was replaced by the visitation of the sick, which appears even in Puritan documents. In the eighteenth century, anointing of the sick reappeared among the Church of the Brethren and has remained an important practice for them.

Refusing to call something a sacrament, then, does not mean abolishing it. In modern times, all seven function in various ways in many churches. One could wish for the freedom of the first centuries of Christianity, when precision of definition was not so important. After all, who is counting when experiencing God's grace? Greater freedom would recognize the presence of Christ as commonly experienced in far more ways than seven.

Elsewhere I have suggested categories: the gospel sacraments of baptism and the Lord's Supper; apostolic sacraments, such as penance and healing; and natural sacraments, such as Christian marriage and Christian burial.[57] In this approach, the canon is still open, just as it was for the first twelve centuries.

THE EMERGENCE OF THE CONCEPT OF SACRAMENTALITY

The Enlightenment certainly dampened sacramental life in much of Protestantism in Europe and America. But various changes came in the nineteenth century. A deeper sense of the exchange between the physical and spiritual emerged, partly as a result of the reaction of the Romantic Movement to Enlightenment rationalism, partly because of an evolving sense of social interaction.

One of the pioneers in delineating what we would now call sacramentality was the Anglican F. D. Maurice. In 1837, he published *The Kingdom of Christ* and in 1853 amplified some of its ideas in *Theological Essays*. The *Kingdom of Christ* was addressed to a Quaker and speaks warmly in defense of sacramental forms of worship. Maurice bases his arguments on the basis of both creation and redemption. God has created the universe; therefore, the physical is a means of encounter with the divine. There is no gap between the physical and the divine. Each leads to the other, so we find God in the material world and this, in turn, reeks of divinity.[58]

An important consequence of Maurice's sacramental thinking was that he realized the consequences of sacraments for social justice. If the material world reflects the face of God, then so does one's neighbor. Sacraments, since they are material, relate us not just to God but to our fellow humans. Our unity with one another, celebrated in the sacraments, also unites us with all our fellow creatures. Sacraments lead us to work for justice because the kingdom of Christ does not stop at church doors but leads to all the world outside.

More than any other Western Christian of the time, Maurice saw the ethical consequences of the sacraments. His influence was magnified through actions such as founding a Working Men's College in 1854 and in establishing cooperative societies to improve the economic status of workers. The Quakers had made connections between worship and social justice much earlier, but they were not concerned about sacraments. Maurice showed just how worldly the sacraments were, and many Anglicans became involved in crusades for social justice on the basis of his insights concerning the unity of sacramental worship and social action.

In the twentieth century, two other Anglican priests developed some of these ideas. Percy Dearmer is probably most remembered for his attention to liturgical niceties and aesthetics as related to the so-called English Use. He made enormous contributions to English hymnody, partly through work with the composer Ralph Vaughan Williams. But Dearmer was also thoroughly aware of the ethical concerns of the sacraments. He sensed the irony of the use of vestments produced by sweat labor, the mockery of church furnishings produced by the underpaid.[59]

The other divine was A. G. Hebert, who spent most of his life in the Society of the Sacred Mission at Kelham, England. His greatest monument was the book *Liturgy and Society* (1935), which led to his editing *The Parish Communion* (1937). Strongly influenced by Swedish Lutheran theologians, the German Benedictines at Maria Laach, and F. D. Maurice, Hebert sought to show how the sacraments overcome corrosive individualism and cement Christians together in the body of Christ. But the world also belongs to Christ, and the sacraments enable Christians to continue their ministry in the world in Christ's name. The Body of Christ was to be realized in both church and world.[60]

The 1950s and 1960s saw a growing sense of the importance of sacramentality as a dimension of Christianity. Theologians as different as Dietrich Bonhoeffer and George MacLeod pointed to the sacraments and their relationship to the doctrine of creation. The lines between church and world were being erased. I reflected these currents, three decades ago, by writing, "I offer this sin-stained world of politics in the eucharist and am given back the same world, but now I understand it to be Christ's world."[61] The words "this is my body" also mean "this is my precinct," "this is my district." George MacLeod warned us against being more spiritual than God.

The 1970s brought a new dimension to our thinking about sacraments, largely from the world outside the church. This was the environmental movement, and it often confronted Christianity with being the source of evil in urging conquest and dominion over nature. Some Christians sincerely believed that the natural world was for humans to exploit and that dominion and control (Gen. 1:28) meant liberty to do whatever was profitable rather than what involved stewardship.

Through a process of research and teaching, science has gradually made most of the public, Christian or not, aware of how mutually interdependent we are with nature. The eradication of species diminishes us all. Global warming threatens humanity, not just those with an affluent lifestyle but rich and poor alike. We are all affected by the same climate and whatever actions of humans change it.

As a result, Christians have rediscovered the basic doctrine of creation. It is humbling to realize how much our liturgical life has neglected the creation story in favor of the redemptive story although this is not so in early and Eastern rites. Scholars have even speculated that the loss of any reference to creation in the Western eucharist, Catholic or Protestant, may be one reason the West has led the way in the conquest of nature instead of celebrating our consanguinity with the created world. It is not accidental that recent eucharistic rites in the West have remedied a thousand-year neglect and now usually begin with commemoration of creation before proceeding to narrate redemption. Creation now seems the logical place to begin in considering the nature of sacramentality.

An excellent example of current thought is a recent book by the Anglican theologian John Macquarrie, *A Guide to the Sacraments*. His opening chapter takes its title from a book published in 1940 by the then Archbishop of Canterbury, William Temple, "A Sacramental Universe." Macquarrie argues that because God "is universally present, there is, shall we say, a sacramental potentiality in virtually everything."[62] And Macquarrie acknowledges that poets have often grasped this insight before theologians. He quotes lines from Elizabeth Barrett Browning:

> Earth's crammed with heaven,
> And every common bush afire with God.

Sacramentality is everywhere, but we need the gift to see it.

CHAPTER TWO

Baptism in Practice and Controversy

In Luther's monumental tract of 1520, the *Babylonian Captivity*, the only sacrament to remain unscathed was that of baptism. He praises God that God has "preserved in his church this sacrament at least, untouched and untainted by the ordinances of men, and has made it free to all nations and classes of mankind, and has not permitted it to be oppressed by the filthy and godless monsters of greed and superstition."[1] Luther waxes lyric in praise of this sacrament, although the tract does give him an occasion to make a negative crack about monastic vows.

This relative tranquility was not to last long. Indeed, the very next year, controversy was to arise over baptism, and Luther was to spend the rest of his life defending infant baptism. He was aware that shifts were underway in current baptismal practice. He probably did not realize just what major transitions in baptismal practice and theologies had been in process in the West, but Luther's time saw the final evolution in some baptismal practices that had been slowly unraveling for centuries.

THE EVOLUTION OF MEDIEVAL BAPTISM

Luther must have been most familiar with recent changes in the mode of baptizing infants. The prevailing mode for centuries in West and East had been total immersion or dipping of the infant. The size of medieval fonts in the West accommodated dipping the naked infant in the water. Sprinkling was known to Aquinas in the thirteenth century but immersion still predominated.[2] But by Luther's time, immersion was becoming the exception rather than the rule. Here Luther is clearly the conservative; his *Babylonian Captivity* explains, "I would have those who are to be baptized completely immersed in the water, as the word says and as the mystery indicates."[3] His rites for baptism of 1523 and 1526 specify in the rubrics "dip him in the font" or "dip it in the font."[4] He even did a linguistic analysis in 1519 to show that the German word for baptism came from the word for deep. Baptism signifies that "the old man and the sinful birth of flesh and blood are to be wholly drowned" and baptism should be "a true and complete sign of the thing it signifies."[5] *Signifying* becomes an important part of his argument in addition to *causing*. At least briefly, Zwingli agreed that immersion was to reflect dying and rising with Christ (Rom. 6:3-5), but eventually he and most of the Reformed agreed that the central sign was washing, not death and resurrection. Pouring became the norm.[6]

Luther may not have been aware of it, but other momentous shifts had gone on already in the process of Christian initiation in the West and one stage was in its final act. This was the disintegration of the unity of initiation, still preserved in the East, where one goes through the whole process at one time whether as infant or as adult. The three chief acts of initiation—water baptism, confirmation, and first communion—had been rent asunder by extraneous forces. The final shattering was the separation of confirmation from baptism. Elizabeth I was born on September 7, 1533, and baptized and confirmed three days later.[7] But this became impossible after both the first *Book of Common Prayer* of 1549 and the Catechism of Trent of 1566 deemed confirmation inexpedient before the age of seven.

The other fracture was the earlier dissociation of baptism from communion in the West. Before the twelfth century, infants in the West were given communion of the wine, as they still are in the East. But growing scrupulosity over the danger of spilling the blood of Christ led to the suspension of communion with wine by anyone, including the sick, except for priests. The result was that in the West infant communion had ceased in most places by the twelfth century, although it was not formally ended until the Council of Trent, while acknowledging the earlier practice, effectually refuted it in 1562.[8]

Thus the rite in the ritual books Luther knew was simply the isolated act of baptism, severed from confirmation and communion by an interval of years. One other mooring had been lost, too, the connection between baptism and the paschal season with its reenactment of the death and resurrection of Christ. As early as the third century, Tertullian in North Africa and murals in a house church in Dura-Europos on the eastern frontier of the empire had associated baptism with the death and resurrection of Christ. At the church in Dura-Europos, built in 232 and destroyed in 256, the wall painting next to the font is of the three Marys going to the tomb on Easter morning.

For centuries, infants were baptized at the Easter or Pentecostal vigils. If they lived near a cathedral this would be performed by the bishop on those occasions. Increasingly, fear developed over infants dying unbaptized if they delayed baptism. The doctrine of original sin, especially after Augustine (who was not baptized until he was thirty), led to an urgency for speedy baptism. The child who died unbaptized would forfeit a chance of heaven. So baptism became normal within eight days of birth, at any time of year, and was presided over by a priest. Any paschal sense had been lost in the process, and baptism for the remission of the guilt of original sin became the central theological theme of the sacrament.

Infants do not have an opportunity to commit actual sin. But by Luther's time, except for Jews and Muslims, there were no unbaptized adults left in Europe. His two baptismal rites are for the baptism of infants. It is not until 1662 that the Church of England found it necessary to concoct a rite of baptism for "Those of Riper Years," as if this were the exception to the norm, "The Order of Baptism both Publick and Private." In terms of practice, infant baptism had been normative for a thousand years except on the fringes of Christendom.

Furthermore, the fear of infants dying unbaptized often led to baptism by midwives in the birth room. This must have been common since Calvin rails against baptism by women.[9] Women must have performed a significant number of baptisms in medieval Europe. Baptism by laypeople has always been considered valid ever since Tertullian said, "That which is received on equal terms can be given on equal terms."[10] Baptism has long been a lay possibility although many Protestants have clericalized it.

LUTHER'S BAPTISMAL PIETY

Luther's greatest contribution in the area of baptism is one that his descendants still have not fully appropriated, although there are some signs this is changing. Luther has what we may call a baptismal spirituality or, to use the traditional Protestant term, baptismal piety. For Luther, baptism eloquently fulfills his vision of a sacrament as a promise accompanied by a sign.

In "The Holy and Blessed Sacrament of Baptism," Luther declares "there is no greater comfort on earth" than baptism.[11] Baptism remains as a lifelong assurance that "I am baptized, and through my baptism God, who cannot lie, has bound himself in a covenant with me."[12] Baptism is a way of life, abiding in the knowledge that one's sins are forgiven. It is "so great, gracious, and full of comfort, we should . . . ceaselessly, joyfully, and from the heart thank, praise, and honor God for it."[13] The Christian life is a "continual remembrance of this promise made to us in baptism."[14] For centuries, Lutheran fonts were placed at the front of the church to remind worshipers of their baptism.

The Christian life is lived in the aftermath of baptism, and this event remains a lifelong comfort or consolation. Luther could find the courage to live through each day by reminding himself that he was baptized. When sin or conscience weights us down, "we must retort, 'But I am baptized.'"[15] So the "Christian life is nothing else than a daily Baptism."[16] Penance is simply a return to baptism. Above all, baptism is the reassurance that we belong to God and that God's action in baptizing us is a promise effective for the rest of our lives.

But baptism does imply the presence of faith, and this was to lead to problems. Early on, Luther simply asserted that "infants are aided by the faith of others, namely, those who bring them for baptism."[17] Later on, he asserted that "we pray God to grant him [the child] faith. But we do not baptize him on that account, but solely on the command of God."[18] Luther is not troubled by the problem of finding faith in an infant.

Baptism is intimately connected with the forgiveness of sin for Luther. Throughout life, penance is a return to baptism. Penance is not the second plank after shipwreck (sin) for the ship of baptism is still afloat and we may return to it again and again. Therefore the Christian life is one long living out of one's baptism, to which one can return with hope and confidence.

34

Baptism was also directly related to the death and resurrection of Christ. For this reason, as we have seen, Luther prefers the sign-act of immersion. But in his baptismal rites of 1523 there is an even more cosmic dimension. For the central theological statement of the rite, he assembled his famous flood prayer, which relates God's use of water in cleansing the world through Noah and the ark, the deliverance of the Jews from slavery through the Red Sea, and the baptism of Jesus in the Jordan. Water serves now for "a rich and full washing away of sins."[19]

Baptism was so much a summation of the gospel that Luther found it necessary to produce his "Order of Baptism" in German in 1523, preceding by three years the publication of his German Mass. His baptismal rite contains most of the medieval ceremonies even though he declares them unnecessary. Three years later, he published "The Order of Baptism Newly Revised." Gone are some of the purity ceremonies such as blowing on the child, giving of salt, one exorcism, the anointing of the ears, and the two anointings of the head. Most of these ceremonies have biblical roots—blowing refers to the Holy Spirit, as does salt; the effetha, touching the ears and mouth (Mark 7:34), to hearing and speaking the Word; the candle to Matthew 25:1-3; the garment to Galatians 3:27. Both of Luther's rites are emphatically for children, the Gospel reading being Mark 10:13-16: "People were bringing little children to him." There are several parallels in these two rites to the changes in ceremonies in the Roman Ritual before and after Vatican II. In our time, the flood prayer has been widely admired and imitated in other churches.

THE RELATION OF BAPTISM TO FAITH

It did not take long for others to question some of the more traditional views of Luther, especially the baptism of infants. In late December of 1521, just after Christmas, Luther being out of town, three radicals from Zwickau appeared in Wittenberg and argued against infant baptism on the basis of Mark 16:16 ("The one who believes and is baptized . . ."). A radical priest, Thomas Müntzer, soon picked up their challenge to infant baptism and raised serious questions about the baptism of children. His voice was silenced in his defeat and death in the Peasants' War of 1524–1525.

A more lasting challenge soon appeared in Zurich in 1525. A reformation was underway there, led by the priests Ulrich Zwingli and Leo Jud. The city magistrates had sided with these reformers, and important changes in the liturgical life of the city had been in progress. But soon a group arose who found that Zwingli's teaching pointed beyond where he was willing to go himself. The chief issue was the baptism of infants. A group of what were to be known as the Swiss Brethren challenged Zwingli in public disputations on this issue on January 10 and 17, 1525. Zwingli was supported by the City Council, which decreed that infant baptism should continue. Almost immediately (January 21, 1525) in a private home, a layman, Conrad Grebel, rebaptized the priest George Blaurock. The day became recognized as "the birthday of Anabaptism."[20] The term *Anabaptists* means "rebaptizers" and was applied by their opponents to a wide range of movements with many common practices but a variety of theological positions. Persecution turned many of them into martyrs. The groups surviving today are Mennonites, Amish, and Hutterites.

Successive disputations in March and November 6-8, 1525, failed to move the City Council, and with grim humor it decreed death by drowning to those who rebaptized. But adherents continued to grow in number. In nearby Waldshut, a priest named Balthasar Hubmaier was rebaptized the day before Easter 1525 and proceeded to rebaptize over three hundred of his flock, using a milk pail and ordinary water from the town fountain.[21] Here was the sacred in the form of the ordinary, and the ancient font was eventually thrown into the Rhine. It is characteristic of the Anabaptists that the mode was pouring, not immersion.

Hubmaier staunchly defended baptism of believers only. He produced a rite for believers' baptism in 1527, shortly before he was martyred. After baptism, the presider (bishop) lays hands on the head of the new member, recognizing him or her "as a member participating in the use of her keys, breaking bread and praying with other Christian sisters and brothers."[22] For those within the community, there was also an exit, the ban. Hubmaier provides a form for the ban based on Matthew 18:15-18 and 1 Corinthians 5, consigning the offender "to the devil for the destruction of the flesh so that the spirit might be saved on the day of the Lord Jesus."[23]

The ideal was a church kept pure by careful admission and continuing scrutiny of those admitted through baptism. Only the mature were ready for admission. One leader, Hans Hut, proposed that only those thirty years of age, like Jesus, could be baptized. The purpose of the ban and subsequent shunning was the hope that reform would ensue and the offender be readmitted with laying on of hands. Thus only a pure church could celebrate the Lord's Supper. There were debates about the severity of shunning, especially within a marriage.

Many of the early Anabaptists were martyred in short order since it was widely recognized that they represented a challenge to the established relation of church and state. A leader in the 1530s was the Dutch priest Menno Simons. In his "Foundation of Christian Doctrine" (1539), he gave a classic statement of the arguments against infant baptism. First, on the basis of scripture, he argued that in the two favorite texts for baptism (Matt. 28:19 and Mark 16:16), the commands to make disciples and to believe precede the command to baptize. He argued that the New Testament knows no baptism of infants and therefore infant baptism is unscriptural.

A second argument was that "young children are without understanding and unteachable; therefore baptism cannot be administered to them without perverting the ordinance of the Lord, misusing His exalted name and doing violence to His Holy Word."[24] Baptism of infants is unreasonable since they cannot understand what is at stake. Forcefully, Menno contradicted Luther's assertion that faith is dormant in children. Therefore, only believers were to be baptized. This was deemed in accord with both scripture and reason.

Zwingli, of course, had already responded in the midst of the disputations of 1525. He compared baptism to the covenant of God with Israel. Circumcision for him was a clear parallel. "Baptism," he says, "is simply a mark or pledge by which those who receive it are dedicated to God." It marks the baptized as a member of a community and therefore is a public seal or mark of his or her inclusion in the community of faith. Zwingli decries water as an effectual sign, even suggesting the Anabaptists make too much of its efficacy, but he does insist on the importance of marking the limits of the community of faith. A pledge or seal is an important factor in building up the community. Zwingli's reference to baptism as dedication may be the earliest use of this interpretation.[25]

Many Anabaptists spoke of three types of baptism, Spirit, water, and blood, from a favorite text, 1 John 5:6-8. The growth in the inner spiritual life led to baptism in water and this frequently led to suffering and bloodshed. Baptism in the Spirit might be sudden or a slow process, freeing a person from sin. Baptism in water announced one's fellowship with the community that recognized one's Spirit baptism. Baptism in blood was the terrible reality of suffering and affliction which ensued.[26]

Various Anabaptist theologians had their individual contributions. Pilgram Marpeck, for example, favored the dedication of infants in a public ceremony. In common, the Anabaptists agreed that the New Testament bore no witness to the baptism of infants and that circumcision was not a relevant parallel. They argued that baptism without prior faith was contrary to scripture. They were motivated by an intense sense of the community of the truly baptized. The true church must be kept pure and only the regenerate were admitted. Faithfulness often led to martyrdom. Women were not clergy, but many were martyred.

The Anabaptists were and have remained small in number and usually in situations in which rigorous moral standards can be expected and maintained. But a momentous change was on the horizon as the seventeenth century dawned. Undoubtedly there was influence from Anabaptists. But what was to become the Baptist movement soon took on distinctive characteristics of its own.

John Smyth was a priest of the Church of England who, growing impatient of reform in the national church, withdrew with a band of followers to Amsterdam in 1608, the same year another Anglican priest, John Robinson, led his followers, the future Pilgrims, to the Netherlands and eventually to Leiden. Smyth, through his contact with Dutch Mennonites, came to be increasingly persuaded that only believers' baptism was genuine, and he rebaptized himself in 1609. The same year, those who followed him formed what is recognized as the first Baptist church. The same ideas were brought back to England in 1612, the year of Smyth's death, by one of his followers, Thomas Helwys. There, Helwys established the first Baptist church in England. Roger Williams organized the first Baptist congregation in America in 1639. From these modest beginnings sprang some of the largest Protestant denominations.

Two distinctive practices came to characterize the Baptist process of initiation. "The laying on of hands in immediate connection with baptism was widely practised among Baptists in the seventeenth century, both in Britain and in the American colonies."[27] This died out in time except in Scandinavia. The incentive seems to have been the accounts in Acts of laying on of hands as a sign of the gift of the Holy Spirit.

The other practice, of much more lasting duration, was the insistence on total immersion as the only proper mode of baptism. For Anabaptists, pouring was the preferred pattern and has remained so for most of them. But by the mid-seventeenth century, most Baptists had agreed that immersion was the only biblical pattern and hence the only one allowable.

The Baptist movement grew in England and North America and became widespread throughout the world as the result of missionary activities. The appeal of believers' baptism was broadened by the Enlightenment with its disdain of anything that seemed supernatural. It seemed most rational for faith to precede baptism; there was no need to appeal to the operation of grace within an infant. Believers' baptism was simply a sign of faith to which an individual could give his or her own testimony. Anything supernatural was firmly located in biblical times and not the present.

It is not surprising that almost all of the major religious movements on the American frontier accepted believers' baptism rather than infant baptism.[28] Methodists, Presbyterians, and Congregationalists fought valiantly to persuade people that infant baptism was both biblical and rational. The appeal of a millennium and a half of tradition probably had little impact, but scores of tracts advocating or refuting infant baptism were widely distributed by both sides.[29] The arguments hardly advanced the discussion from the views of the sixteenth century.

Thus, one by one, such movements as the Disciples of Christ, Churches of Christ, Mormons, Seventh-Day Adventists, and others chose believers' baptism. The result is that for most Christians in the southern states of the U.S.A., believers' baptism by immersion is the most prevalent form of Christian initiation.

The most effective defense of infant baptism came from a New England Congregational pastor, Horace Bushnell of Hartford, Connecticut. The prevailing pattern of much of American Christianity was a focus on revivalism, which tended to ignore children until they were of sufficient age for conversion. Then, they would be converted and baptized. But the children of Christians, Bushnell argued, are already Christian from their birth onwards. In essence, Christians, contrary to what Tertullian wrote, are born not made. In his famous book *Christian Nurture* (1847), Bushnell argued that "the child is to grow up a Christian, and never know himself as being otherwise."[30] He speaks of the environment of faith as present in Christian families. Hence one need not wait until a conversion experience but can baptize infants since they are already within the community of faith. In a sense, it is a reiteration of Luther's assertion that the child is assisted by the faith of others, but Bushnell insists it is in the context of family nurture that one becomes Christian. A large number of Christians today would acknowledge that they became Christians through nurture rather than through a conscious conversion experience.

The debate continues in the twentieth century. Without doubt, the most influential statement of the believers' baptism position came from the Swiss theologian Karl Barth although his own church had always practiced infant baptism. In 1943, Barth gave a lecture to theological students on baptism which was soon published in German. Five years later an English translation appeared as *The Teaching of the Church Regarding Baptism*. It was quickly recognized as the leading antipedobaptist statement in the century. If one accepts Barth's opening assertion that baptism "is in essence the representation (*Abbild*) of a man's renewal through his participation by means of the power of the Holy Spirit in the death and resurrection of Jesus Christ,"[31] then one has to accept his conclusion. Only a mature person can respond to such an image. Baptism, hence, is cognitive, not causative.[32] He argued that baptism of infants "is necessarily clouded baptism" and ought to be discontinued though he would not advocate rebaptism of those already baptized. Barth dismissed arguments from the New Testament of household baptisms and the defenses of the reformers.

A forceful reply to Barth came from his colleague Oscar Cullmann, asserting that baptism is causative in that it places a person within the community where faith becomes a possibility rather than simply informing that person of something.[33] Christ equated his baptism and his death (Mark 10:38 and Luke 12:50). Cullmann insisted that, potentially, Christ died for all. This is actualized when one is incorporated into the church, where the possibility of growing up in a community of faith is realized.

A more historical debate went on between two German Lutheran New Testament scholars, both of whom supported the practice of infant baptism. Joachim Jeremias argued that there was indirect proof within the New Testament itself that whole families were baptized at once. Kurt Aland argued that the New Testament evidence did not support this and that not until the third century is there definite proof of the baptism of infants (Tertullian and Hippolytus).[34]

40

Recent years have seen a scrambling of positions with even some Roman Catholics decidedly negative about their own practice of infant baptism.[35] Indeed, in 1980 Rome found it advisable to put out an *Instruction on Infant Baptism* which is defensive about the need to continue baptizing infants when there is a "well-founded hope that the baptism will bear fruit" through a "Christian upbringing."[36] On the other hand, Baptists have criticized their own practice, especially in light of the growing number of baptisms of preschool children. There are problems in regarding one's offspring as outside the church.

The current situation is probably best articulated in the Faith and Order Paper no. 111 of the World Council of Churches, *Baptism, Eucharist and Ministry* (1982). No resolution is attempted, but it advised that

> believer baptists and those who practice infant baptism should reconsider certain aspects of their practices. The first may seek to express more visibly the fact that children are placed under the protection of God's grace. The latter must guard themselves against the practice of apparently indiscriminate baptism and take more seriously their responsibility for the nurture of baptized children to mature commitment of Christ.[37]

Obviously, both sides can profit from major reforms in practice.

THE MODE OF BAPTISM

We have touched briefly on some of the ways that baptism has been performed, but it is worth sorting out some factors that are far more than just mechanical necessities. Indeed, there have been vehement controversies over the mode of baptism, so that some groups have claimed that only their own mode of baptism is valid, often on the basis of scriptural interpretation.

We have already seen that Luther defended the practice of immersion although he realized that it was already slipping away. Today we would speak in terms of the fullness of sign value. Luther, since he thought of baptism largely in terms of forgiveness of sin, wanted to highlight the element of cleansing and washing. Obviously, this is more graphic with an abundance of water than with a shortage. His flood prayer speaks of the baptism of Christ as having consecrated "the Jordan and *all water* as a salutary flood and a rich and full washing away of sins."[38] Along this line, immersion also signifies the cleansing from our past life. So "we should . . . do justice to its meaning and make baptism a true and complete sign of the thing it signifies."[39] The sacramental nature of all water is highlighted in the flood prayer.

At the same time, baptism is a sign of death and resurrection. Luther quotes the familiar Romans 6:3-5 about being buried and rising with Christ. Immersion signifies death; drawing forth signifies life. "It is far more forceful to say that baptism signifies that we die in every way and rise to eternal life, than to say that it signifies merely that we are washed clean of sins."[40] Thus the two images of cleansing and death and resurrection build on each other.

Initially Luther's position on immersion was replicated in Zurich in Leo Jud's *German Baptismal Book* of 1523.[41] But Luther's conservatism did not prevail there nor eventually did it prevail elsewhere. In Strasbourg, water was to be poured on the child. Calvin declares that the mode is not essential but local customs should be followed:

> But whether the person being baptized should be wholly immersed, and whether thrice or once, whether he should only be sprinkled with poured water—these details are of no importance, but ought to be optional to churches according to the diversity of countries. Yet the word "baptize" means to immerse, and it is clear that the rite of immersion was observed in the ancient church.[42]

This is characteristic of Calvin's position that customs may and ought to vary from time to time and place to place. In practice, sprinkling came to prevail in Geneva. This shows a relative freedom in the Reformed Tradition that sets it apart from the Puritan insistence on finding a biblical precedent and making it legally binding.

Once again, conservatism surfaced in the Church of England. The medieval *Sarum Manuale* had a rubric, "*eius baptizet eum sub trina mersione,*" which simply became "shall dip it in the water thrice" in 1549 when Thomas Cranmer assembled the first prayer book of the Church of England. The rest of the rubric was only slightly changed: "First dipping the right side: Second the left side: The third time dipping the face toward the font: So it be discreetly and warily done." But Cranmer added a condition: "And if the child be weak, it shall suffice to pour water upon it, saying the foresaid words, N. I baptize thee, &c."[43]

Still today, the English prayer book specifies "he shall dip it in the Water discreetly and warily" if the godparents "certify him that the Child may well endure it."

But what is prescribed does not always prevail. Charles Wheatly, who wrote the important *Rational Illustration of the Book of Common Prayer* in 1710, tells us that already under Queen Elizabeth I, many parents presented their infants for baptism in fancy gowns and were not about to tolerate dipping.[44] The infants might well endure it but not their finery. One wonders if dipping ever actually functioned in the Church of England. Even English medieval canon law (Lyndwood's *Provinciale*, 1430) had allowed, when it is local custom, sprinkling or pouring on the head alone.

One person who did take this rubric seriously, at least for a while, was John Wesley. While serving a parish in Georgia, he attempted to insist on dipping and his flock thought he was out of his mind. The people won out over the rubric and Wesley later became much more flexible. His 1784 *Sunday Service of the Methodists in North America* provides in the baptism of infants that "he shall dip it in the Water, or sprinkle it therewith" but in the case of "Such as Are of Riper Years" specifies "shall dip him in the Water, or pour Water upon him."[45] Methodists ever since have allowed for immersing, pouring, and sprinkling. Sprinkling is by far the most common mode.

A major cause of contention in the Anglican rite was the provision for making the sign of the cross on the infant's head. In the 1549 prayer book, this involved anointing with oil, but all oil had disappeared in the 1552 revision. There the rubric reads, "the Priest shall make a cross upon the child's forehead."[46] This aroused enormous ire among the Puritan party within the Church of England. In 1603, they complained of "groaning as under a common burden of human rites and ceremonies," and cited "the cross in baptism" as the first item they wished taken away.[47] This did not happen until they took it away themselves in the *Westminster Directory* of 1645: "Baptize the Child with Water . . . by pouring or sprinkling of the water on the face of the Child, without adding any other Ceremony."[48] But dipping and signing with the cross reappeared in the 1662 prayer book of the Church of England.

The Anabaptists saw no need to revert to immersion and baptized with pouring. Hubmaier's use of a milk pail in Waldshut was an eloquent combining of the ordinary and the sacred. Nor did the Baptists differ from this in their early years. By the middle of the seventeenth century, a Baptist chapel was built in a side lane in Tewkesbury, Gloucestershire. A pool was excavated in the floor, making immersion possible, although one suspects the nearby Severn River had been used before.[49] In many instances, natural flowing water was used for immersion (as in the first-century *Didache*) and many early Baptist churches were often situated by and named for local creeks. The Duck River Association of Baptists, for instance, was at one time arrayed against the Elk River Association of Baptists.

While many Baptists have difficulty even using the term *sacrament*, preferring the more legalistic *ordinance*, they express a much more sacramental sense than most pedobaptist churches in insisting on the full sacramental significance of water. Immersion is certainly the most visible outward sign possible. Often, so-called sacramental churches are willing to let the sign slip away in pouring or sprinkling a few drops of water. One must ask who has the deeper sacramental sensibility, those who demand the full sign value of immersion or those who are stingy with water.

There are indications of this shifting today. Other churches have come to realize the importance of signification in the sacraments and many are moving toward immersion, often of both infants and adults. There are approximately a hundred thousand churches in this country with baptismal pools for immersion among Baptists, Disciples of Christ, Churches of Christ, and others. But they are now being joined by various Lutheran, Episcopal, and Roman Catholic parishes from more explicitly sacramental traditions in providing for immersion of all ages. This has developed from felt need on the local parish level rather than by official fiat.[50]

Another group to move in this direction were the various Brethren churches. Springing from both Lutheran and Reformed congregations in Germany in 1708 and with a strong Pietist bent, most moved to America. They were quickly named Dunkards for their insistence on triune immersion, which they adopted because it seemed to them the only biblically warranted practice, along with anointing the sick and footwashing at the Lord's Supper.

Immersion itself soon became a creed for those who professed no creed. Most of the nineteenth-century churches on the American frontier adopted immersion as their normal practice along with believers' baptism. Once again tract warfare erupted, some insisting that no other form of baptism was valid, others being more tolerant. One tract defiantly declares, "IMMERSION IS NOT IN THE BIBLE."[51] As a result of these polemics, not a few people baptized by pouring or sprinkling were eventually rebaptized by immersion. Immersion of believers became the most widely practiced form of baptism in the United States. Especially in the South, those who baptize by any other means are often put on the defensive. It is interesting to see many other churches recognize the full sign value of immersion, if not its biblical warrant.

THE TIME AND PLACE OF BAPTISM

The emphasis on getting the child baptized before it might die had led to baptism's becoming largely a private ceremony. Various medieval canons had decreed that it must occur within eight days of birth. The *Quamprimum* doctrine meant that urgency was important. On family funeral monuments, children who died before baptism are contrasted to those in chrisom robes who made it to the font before they expired.

Luther's rites speak of the "sponsors and others present," yet these rites do not seem to presuppose the presence of a whole congregation. But a major shift comes as the century advances. In Calvin's "Draft Ecclesiastical Ordinances" of 1541 for Geneva, there is a proposal: "Baptism is to take place at the time of Sermon, and should be administered only by ministers or coadjutors.... The stone or baptismal font is to be near the pulpit, in order that there be better hearing for the recitation of this mystery and practice of baptism." Baptism is to occur in the midst of public worship, before the entire congregation. Godparents "of our communion" are to be present.[52]

This meant several major shifts. Emergency baptism is eliminated. Calvin is vociferous in denouncing baptism by women who often baptized in the birth room if the child looked fragile. He goes out of his way to deny that baptism is necessary to salvation, as had been affirmed in the Lutheran Augsburg Confession ("Our churches teach that Baptism is necessary for salvation").[53] God, Calvin says, "adopts our babies as his own before they are born"[54] and again "infants are not barred from the Kingdom of Heaven just because they happen to depart the present life before they have been immersed in water."[55] Children of believers, because of God's promise, already belong to the body of Christ.

According to Calvin, one should not despise or take lightly God's command to baptize but receive it "from those only to whom the Lord has committed" baptism and the eucharist.[56] Calvin thus is more clerical than the Catholic position, which allowed lay administration of baptism even by women. Preachers and teachers of the Word are to administer baptism, and no one else.

The upshot is that baptism is set in the context of the preaching of the Word. Baptism becomes a visible word, a preaching of the gospel itself. Here God's will to save is made visible as well as audible. Without God's word, baptism is only water. Calvin's baptismal and eucharistic rites both cite gospel warrants for the doing of these acts.[57] Baptism is done in the context of a worshiping community, usually on Sunday morning. Thus it is always a public act in which the child is welcomed into the actual community that is present. What came to be normal in many Reformed churches was a metal hoop on the pulpit in which a silver or pewter basin was set for baptism. In later Puritanism these could be quite elaborate.[58] But they were always highly visible so the congregation could participate in the act. Both time and location ensured that baptism was seen by all.

Calvin's concern that baptism be public was reflected in the Church of England, which, nevertheless, made provision for private baptism in the rite "Of Them That Be Baptized in Private Houses in Time of Necessity." Provision is also made for conditional baptism if it is uncertain whether the child is already baptized or not. The 1549 prayer book contains a prayer of blessing for the water in the font, which is to be changed at least monthly; this disappears in 1552.

A rubric in the "Administration of Public Baptism To Be Used in the Church" in both 1549 and 1552 acknowledges that baptism in the early church was administered only at Easter and Whitsunday but that this cannot be recovered. It does, however, require

> that baptism should not be ministered but upon Sundays and other holy days, when the most number of people may come together. As well for that the congregation there present may testify the receiving of them, that be newly baptized, into the number of Christ's Church, as also because in the Baptism of Infants, every man present may be put in remembrance of his own profession made to God in his Baptism.[59]

Baptism thus has a dual function: it welcomes the new Christian but it also reminds the whole congregation of their own baptism. The timing came to be after the last lesson at morning or evening prayer.

A strange bit of conservatism, however, prevailed in the Canons of 1604, which decreed that the font be of stone and "be set up in the ancient usual places," that is, near the door. The Reformed and Lutheran traditions generally preferred a font near the pulpit and altar-table, and the Puritans sought the same. This debate still continues between those who see the dominant symbol of the church as a congregation of people and those who see it as a building. In the American colonies, frequently the font did move to the front of the building in Anglican churches or was simply a basin on the altar-table.[60]

The rite presupposes baptism of infants. Not until 1662 did the Church of England add a rite for "Baptism to Such as Are of Riper Years" as non-Christians were encountered in the New World. Obviously, infant baptism was the norm and adult candidates were treated as exceptions to this norm. John Wesley eliminated the rite for private baptism altogether.

On the American frontier, baptisms frequently occurred at the end of camp meetings, as a harvest of those newly converted. In much of American Protestantism today, baptisms occur on a regular, almost weekly, basis as children are born or adults converted. In some traditions, especially Lutheran, there has been an attempt to focus on baptismal seasons such as Baptism of the Lord, Easter, Pentecost, or All Saints Day. For most of Protestantism, baptism is a public ceremony before the entire Sunday morning congregation. The baptismal font or pool is usually centrally located near the pulpit and altar-table so as to be fully visible both for welcoming new Christians and for reminding others of their own baptisms.

THE PROCESS OF INITIATION

Baptism may be the prime focus of Christian initiation, but baptism alone is not the totality of the process. It is well said that the eucharist is the only part of baptism that is repeated. But ever since the twelfth century in the West, the eucharist has ceased to function as part of baptism and been seen as a separate, distinct act and occasion. In the early church, catechesis, baptism, anointing, and eucharist were seen as a related process. But by the sixteenth century, in the West the integrity of initiation had been shattered and each element functioned in isolation from the others.

Our present purpose is to see what roles, if any, Protestants found for the fragments of catechesis and confirmation before recent attempts to reintegrate the process. By the sixteenth century, catechesis was just a perfunctory act in the baptism of infants who obviously were unteachable. Confirmation was largely a pious option, good if a bishop happened by but usually a rarity. In an archdiocese such as York with over 800 villages, one wonders how many villagers ever even saw a bishop. Stories abound of bishops confirming from horseback as they rode through a village.

It is not surprising that Luther took a dim view of a ceremony desultory in practice and without scriptural warrant. The inherited theology was confused and confusing; it is still common to say that confirmation is a practice looking for a theology. Luther's view in the *Babylonian Captivity* is to the point: confirmation has no scriptural promise and functions as a human invention "to adorn the office of bishops [as] . . . something easy and not too burdensome."[61] Luther produced no rite for confirmation. He insisted that it not be considered a sacrament. Still, in 1523 Luther alluded to confirmation in a sermon: "We do not find fault if every pastor examines the faith of the children to see whether it is good and sincere, lays hands on them, and confirms them."[62] Here in effect, confirmation is a recognition of successful catechesis and confers a blessing.

It is often said that the father of Protestant confirmation is Martin Bucer, reformer of Strasbourg. We presume that he introduced in Strasbourg a practice of examining the children on a Sunday before the congregation as to their knowledge of the catechism. At the end, the pastor stretched his hands over them and blessed them. In other places, Bucer's church order specifically mentions admitting the catechumens "to the table of the Lord" after laying hands on them. For Cologne, Bucer and Melanchthon prepared a "Consultation" for an abortive reformation there. It included a rite of "Confirmation of Children Baptized and Solemn Profession of Their Faith in Christ, and of Their Obedience to be Showed to Christ and to His Congregation." After answering a series of questions, hands are laid on the children with the prayer "Confirm this thy servant with thy Holy Spirit, that he may continue in the obedience of thy gospel."[63]

For the Anabaptists, the problem did not arise since only those who could profess faith were able to receive baptism. The same pertained to Baptists, although some English Baptists did accompany baptism by the laying on of hands. But this did not endure long.

Calvin's position reflects Bucer's practice. He argues that confirmation has been used to devalue baptism and is no true sacrament. Any suggestion that it is necessary to salvation is nonsense. The true practice would be a "catechizing, in which children or those near adolescence would give an account of their faith before the church."[64] A child of ten is envisioned as the ideal candidate and Calvin wrote several catechetical works for this purpose. After public examination, Calvin says, "I warmly approve . . . [of the] laying on of hands, which is simply done as a form of blessing, and wish that it were today restored to pure use."[65]

The Anglican situation moved within a similar orbit, though under more traditional circumstances. Confirmation remained an act of the bishop, but rubrics denied that it was necessary for salvation. It was appended to "A Catechism, That is to say, an instruction to be learned of every child, before he be brought to be confirmed of the bishop." Thus the rite had much of the character of a graduation exercise, as in Bucer and Calvin. In 1549, the children are signed on the forehead; that disappears in 1552. One can see a sacramental intention in 1549 in the formula "confirm and strengthen them with the inward unction of thy holy ghost."[66] Those words disappeared in 1552, although another prayer for the sevenfold gifts of the Holy Spirit remained. A major emphasis was being placed on preparing the child for confirmation by learning the catechism.

The Puritans argued against confirmation as "superfluous" and wanted it taken away. They, did, however, champion the education of children and when they came into power found it useful to have children make public profession of faith before the whole community when of sufficient age. In Massachusetts, this meant accepting the covenant of the local church, which then admitted one to communion. In succeeding generations, as piety slackened, it became a question whether parents who had not owned the covenant could have their children baptized. This was resolved in the Half-Way Covenant practice of allowing that the children be baptized but the parents not commune.

John Wesley removed confirmation from his service book of 1784 but did insist on a "new birth" through a conscious conversion experience. This could come at any time in life's journey and was a rather subjective ratification of what was done for one in baptism. In 1864, the Methodist Episcopal Church instituted a "Form for Receiving

Persons into the Church after Probation"[67] for those baptized adults who had passed a six-month probationary period. Thus for a long time church membership and baptism were not synonymous. This unbiblical anomaly was being rectified at the end of the twentieth century.

By the late twentieth century, the term *confirmation* has been reappropriated by Lutherans and Methodists. Only Anglicans still insist on it being performed by a bishop, though this is no longer necessary for adult converts to Catholicism. New trends are emerging among Methodists, Presbyterians, Episcopalians, and Lutherans, though with different degrees of success.

A common theme is the effort to make initiation complete on one occasion with water baptism being followed by laying on of hands. Communion of children is becoming more and more an issue, as it seems ridiculous to baptize children and immediately excommunicate them. At the same time, it is acknowledged that commitment is a lifelong process. Various ways are proposed to ritualize this reality. Baptismal renewals, affirmations, or reaffirmations can be an annual service including sprinkling the whole assembly. Individuals baptized previously may on their "return home" make a public renewal. Most churches sternly refuse any form of rebaptism, although dissident pastors sometimes perform such an act, as if God had lied in baptism. The congregational baptismal renewal service has overtones of John Wesley's annual Covenant Renewal service although he did not connect it to baptism. Frequently, renewal services are performed at the beginning of the civil year or at Baptism of the Lord Sunday.

At present, several churches are working on models for preparing adults for baptism through a ritualized process of conversion. This owes much to the modern Roman Catholic Rite of Christian Initiation of Adults, which in turn is a recycling of the third-century initiatory process detailed in the *Apostolic Tradition*. By symbolizing the progress in one's faith and understanding through several stages or gates, the whole process is meant to focus on reception of baptism, confirmation, and first communion on Easter Eve or Easter Day.[68]

Clearly many questions are being asked about the whole process by which one becomes a Christian. Baptism of infants does not seem particularly threatened, but a new earnestness about reaching the adult convert is evident. Both United Methodists and Presbyterians have adopted the language of covenant in speaking of baptism. The focus is on entering a community based on covenant, which, of course, was a major theme in the Puritan ecclesiology.

The new rites reflect the Eastern churches in insisting on the integrity of rites in celebration of the whole process of initiation at a single time. They also recover many long-lost elements such as profession of the creed, renunciation of evil, blessing of the water, and laying on of hands. Thus much that is new is very old. As a result, the rites have increasingly become similar.

Some believers'-baptism churches have introduced rites of dedication for infants in which parents pledge to rear them in the faith. Other churches may have services of thanksgiving for the birth or adoption of a child. All seem to sense the need for some form of public profession of faith when a child reaches sufficient age, whether it be known as confirmation or by some other name.

In short, Protestant practices of baptism are still very much in transition as they evolve to respond to new and old problems. One can only marvel at the variety and rich diversity that accompanies these efforts to signify the making of a Christian.

CHAPTER THREE

Baptismal Meanings

W hat is done in baptismal practice and argued over in controversies obviously both reflects and shapes what this sacrament
means. Practice often forms the basis of reflection; reflection frequently shapes practice. So the two are intimately connected even though we
may be looking at somewhat different types of evidence in each case.

It is time now to seek out various expressions of what Protestants,
over the course of five centuries, have found to be the meaning of what
they did or observed in baptism. Our evidence is chiefly in two forms:
theological treatises and the rites themselves. Each tells us what is
experienced or intended to be experienced in baptism. We shall use
both genres in ferreting out what baptism meant to different groups at
different times and places.

The reformers believed they were following scripture and it was
cited constantly in all discussions. Baptism is mentioned much more
frequently in the New Testament than the eucharist, a fact not surprising in a missionary situation. We shall structure what follows on
the basis of five chief metaphors for baptism there. By no means are
these the only images for baptism found in the New Testament; there
are many peripheral metaphors, such as naming the name of Christ,
sealing, the royal priesthood, putting on Christ, and others.

At the same time, baptism in the New Testament is in an eschatological context, beginning with the baptism of John the Baptist in the eschatological urgency of his preaching for repentance: "Repent, for the kingdom of heaven has come near" (Matt. 3:3). Baptism is done in the expectation of the nearness of the kingdom. Occasionally, entire families were baptized as a unit so that none would be left behind (1 Cor. 1:16; Acts 16:15, 33; 18:8). Baptism gives entrance to the kingdom: "no one can enter the kingdom of God without being born of water and Spirit" (John 3:5). So we shall explore first just how much this context of eschatology was recovered.

In our analysis, the chief New Testament metaphors for baptism are five: forgiveness of sin; union to Christ, especially in His death and resurrection; incorporation into the church; reception of the Holy Spirit; and new birth or regeneration. The minor images do not seem to have caught the imagination of the church over the centuries to the extent that these five have.

These five are by no means in opposition to each other. Frequently they overlap; always they complement each other. In most of the sources we shall study, many if not all of them appear. None of them is used exclusively. Our task is to sort out the centers of gravity. For whom does forgiveness of sin become the dominant image? Why does incorporation into the church appear more significant for another? Even in so doing, we must realize that the emphasis is relative. By focusing on the most important metaphors we do not mean to suggest that the others have been relinquished. Often they are simply in the background but still in the picture. So it will not be necessary to list all five metaphors in each discussion, only those in the foreground. We conclude with a few words on baptism and social justice.

THE ESCHATOLOGICAL DIMENSION

It is not surprising that an eschatological emphasis on the last things comes in times of crisis and persecution. Among the Anabaptists, we see this theme in the sixteenth century. The radical reformation of the Anabaptists broke with the principalities and powers of the existing age. With few exceptions, the magistrates were their enemies, not their protectors. Anabaptists were "bent upon either the restoration of the primitive church or the assembling of a new church, all in an eschatological mood far more intense than anything to be found in normative Protestantism or Catholicism."[1]

The Anabaptists were living in the latter days and so could defy the powers of the age. Thus they could denounce the conventional baptism of infants and call for a fresh repentance just as John the Baptist denounced those who presumed for their salvation because "we have Abraham as our ancestor" (Matt. 3:9). The signs of the times were apparent to them in the presence of the Holy Spirit in their assemblies. The institutions of both church and state were under judgment as part of this fallen world. Anabaptists could reordain priests who joined their movement as if official channels of grace no longer operated.

Baptism, then, became the sign of moving into a new age in which one was already a part of the oncoming kingdom. One became part of a new order of creation as a member of a tightly disciplined community. And baptism functioned as the sign of that transition from the old order to the new. The one being baptized received the keys of the kingdom as he or she moved into a reconstituted church. Baptism prepared a person to be a citizen of the coming kingdom of God on earth.

Similar eschatological themes appear much later in groups with great apocalyptic hopes. The Adventist movement in the nineteenth century led the members of what became the Adventist Christian Church and the Seventh-Day Adventist Church to see baptism in the context of preparation for the imminent second coming of Christ, especially as depicted in John 14:1-3 and Revelation 19. Mormons practice baptism for the dead (1 Cor. 15:29) in anticipation of the end of time. For Pentecostals, water baptism is entrance into a community where the Holy Spirit is dramatically at work. It is an already and not yet situation.

Gradually, eschatological ideas are finding their way into mainline churches. *Baptism, Eucharist and Ministry* speaks of baptism as "a sign of the Kingdom of God and of the life of the world to come." Baptism anticipates the day when all will confess the lordship of Jesus Christ.[2] In various ways, new rites hint at the eschatological dimension. The United Methodist baptism rite prays that those being baptized "may share in his [Christ's] final victory."[3] The Lutheran service speaks of leading "*godly lives* until the day of Jesus Christ."[4] And Presbyterians may pray in thanksgiving over the water, "Strengthen *them* to serve you with joy / until the day you make all things new."[5]

It seems that the eschatological context of baptism will be articulated more in the future just as eschatology has been recovered in recent years in the eucharist.

THE FORGIVENESS OF SIN

We begin our survey of the five chief New Testament metaphors of baptismal meaning with the most obvious natural sign of baptism, that of cleansing, washing, or forgiveness of sin. It was already present in the baptism of John and in numerous groups such as the Essenes as well as in many non-Judaic religions. Acts represents Peter as saying, "Repent, and be baptized every one of you in the name of Jesus Christ so that your sins may be forgiven" (2:38) and the same concept is repeated in Acts 22:16 and 1 Corinthians 6:11. Both 1 Peter 3:21 and Hebrews 10:22 compare baptism with an outward washing and the inward cleansing of "a good conscience." The concept became dogma in the Nicene Creed: "One baptism for the remission of sins."

It became a staple of Christian reflection on baptism. After the fourth century, forgiveness of sins was reinforced by the concept that children bore the guilt of original sin, transmitted, as it were, in the genes of Adam. Baptism was seen as canceling the guilt of original sin though not the propensity to sin. It also removed the guilt of the actual sin that anyone of accountable age had committed. It is not strange, then, that the dominant medieval mode of understanding baptism had become largely, if not exclusively, that of forgiveness of sin. By the late Middle Ages, "it became established everywhere that all infants should be baptized not later than the eighth day after birth"[6] for fear that salvation was impossible without it. The John 3:5 threat of risking the kingdom if one was not baptized applied to all ages.

This view makes it clear that God acts in baptism. Baptism is an effective sign. One enters into a new relationship with the divine through baptism. Thus one of the defenses of infant baptism is that God enters into a covenant relationship with infants and forgives the inherited corruption of our race. This implies that baptism is causative and not simply cognitive.

Given the medieval emphasis on baptism as forgiveness, it is not strange that this should be Luther's dominant image. It underlies his arguments for immersion as signifying "that the old man and the sinful birth of flesh and blood are to be wholly drowned by the grace of

God."[7] Baptism is seen as a great comfort in providing the knowledge that God has forgiven our sin. "In baptism a person becomes guiltless, pure, and sinless, while at the same time continuing full of evil inclinations." In baptism, God has entered into a covenant relationship not to "count my sin against me."[8] We can live our life in confidence of this forgiveness until death.

The divine promise which radiates here is largely one of forgiveness and acceptance. The sign is effective throughout life. This accounts also for Luther's tying penance to baptism as "nothing but a way and a return to baptism."[9] The Augsburg Confession of 1530 claims that Lutherans "teach that Baptism is necessary for salvation" in the context of defending infant baptism.[10] Through baptism, we are forgiven and our faith in that forgiveness justifies us.

The Anabaptists found much to say about baptism as forgiveness of sin, actual as well as original. The Schleitheim Confession of 1527 states: "Baptism shall be given to all those who have been taught repentance and the amendment of life and [who] believe truly that their sins are taken away through Christ."[11] What, of course, separated Anabaptists from others was that all their candidates were adults and had been catechized and professed repentance. They had consciously and deliberately put the old life behind them and submitted to the rule of Christ.

This is articulated in various ways. According to Conrad Grebel, in baptism "sins have been washed away for him who is baptized, changes his mind, and believes before and after; . . . [baptism] signifies that a man is dead and ought to be dead to sin and walks in newness of life and spirit." These things are impossible for children, who "are saved without faith,"[12] and therefore baptism is not necessary for salvation. Balthasar Hubmaier defines a threefold process of baptism of the Spirit, of water, and of blood. In water baptism, a person "confesses his sins before all people. One also testifies thereby that one believes in the forgiveness of his sins through the death and resurrection of our Lord Jesus Christ."[13] Personal faith in forgiveness is operative in a fashion impossible among infants. Yet sin remains a reality even in the church so that the newly baptized must submit to the community "since fraternal admonition and the Christian ban proceed from such inner, heartfelt and fervent love [that one should] . . . accept such admonition from his brethren in a friendly and kind way, and with thanksgiving."[14]

The metaphor of forgiveness appears in most of the magisterial reformers as well. Zwingli links Christ's baptism closely to that of John the Baptist, namely, a baptism of repentance. On the other hand, Zwingli, clearly nervous about any sense that external actions can affect spiritual states, declares: "It is clear that the external baptism of water cannot effect spiritual cleansing. . . . Baptism cannot save or purify."[15] Only an inward baptism can effect this cleansing, and that comes directly through the operation of the Holy Spirit.

Calvin repudiates Zwingli's limitation of sacraments to a mere "token and mark." He stresses the forgiveness of sin:

> The first thing that the Lord sets out for us is that baptism should be a token and proof of our cleansing; or (the better to explain what I mean) it is like a sealed document to confirm to us that all our sins are so abolished, remitted, and effaced that they can never come to his sight, be recalled, or charged against us. For he wills that all who believe be baptized for the remission of sins.[16]

It is hard to imagine a stronger statement of baptism as remission of sin. Furthermore, it is a lifelong engagement: "At whatever time we are baptized, we are once for all washed and purged for our whole life."[17] Throughout life, we can recall with hope that we have been forgiven in baptism. In it, Christ's purity has been conveyed to us and subsequent sin cannot efface our forgiveness. Baptism is the real sacrament of penance, and throughout life we can take consolation in the cleansing we have received in Christ's blood in baptism.

We are all infected with the contagion of original sin, but baptism removes our condemnation. The perversity still remains. Infants are to be baptized and will grow into "greater zeal for renewal" when they realize what has been done for them in baptism.[18]

The Church of England followed suit in its Articles of Religion, arguing that baptism is more than just "a sign of profession" but that "the promises of the forgiveness of sin, and of our adoption to be the sons of God by the Holy Ghost, are visibly signed and sealed."[19] The Westminster Confession of Faith, the Puritan document of 1647, concurs, listing "remission of sins" among the benefits conferred.[20] John Wesley, in arguing for the great Christian doctrine of original sin, points out that infants demonstrate the presence of original sin. Therefore they are baptized because of their need for remission of sin along with the rest of us. Among the churches insisting on immersion, the obvious symbolism of cleansing frequently comes to the forefront.

In recent documents and rites, the metaphor of forgiveness of sin is prominent. *Baptism, Eucharist and Ministry* lists "Conversion, Pardoning and Cleansing" second under "The Meaning of Baptism." The connection with John's baptism of repentance is mentioned along with New Testament references to baptism as washing and cleansing: "Thus those baptized are pardoned, cleansed and sanctified by Christ" and receive "a new ethical orientation."[21]

The forgiveness of sin receives a prominent role in most recent baptismal rites. In the United Methodist service, the Thanksgiving over the Water prays "to wash away *their* sin / and clothe *them* in righteousness / throughout *their* lives."[22] The Lutheran rite prays: "Wash away the sin of *all those* who *are* cleansed by this water."[23] The Episcopal rite is more terse: the baptized "are cleansed from sin."[24] Presbyterians pray "Wash away the sin of *all* who *are* cleansed by it [water]," having previously noted that "In baptism . . . God frees us from sin and death."[25] Other rites have similar expressions of baptism as effecting forgiveness of sin.

UNION TO CHRIST'S DEATH AND RESURRECTION

The second New Testament metaphor we shall trace is the image of union to Christ himself in his death and resurrection. This has a double significance in relating us both to his life and to his work. We are "baptized into union" with Christ's own death and resurrection (Rom. 6:3) by dying and rising with him through baptism. A similar expression of this union occurs in Colossians 2:12. At the same time, we are united to his priestly ministry. The Christ to whom we are united in baptism is our great high priest (Heb. 9:11) and, as a result, we become a priestly people (1 Pet. 2:9). Thus all believers come to have a common priesthood.

The connection of baptism with death and resurrection has a long history. It is found in the third century with Tertullian in North Africa and visually in the baptistery at Dura-Europos, dated 232–256. Baptism by immersion has a strong reference to burial, and it is not surprising that early baptisteries often imitated the form of a mausoleum. Thus the paschal nature of baptism has deep roots in the Christian imagination. Quite likely, most baptisms by the fourth century occurred at Easter. Lent had become a final period of preparation for the candidates. In the late fourth century, Egeria tells us of baptisms at Easter in Jerusalem.[26]

For reasons of the fear of children dying unbaptized, the connection of baptism and Christ's death and resurrection at Easter was lost in the rush to get the child baptized quickly lest it die first. The gradual surrendering of immersion further attenuated the image of death and resurrection.

Luther frequently sees baptism as a "blessed dying unto sin and a resurrection in the grace of God,"[27] or again "Baptism, then, signifies two things—death and resurrection, that is, full and complete justification."[28] Referring to Romans 6:4, he says death and resurrection are "not [to] be understood only allegorically as the death of sin and the life of grace, as many understand it, but as actual death and resurrection. For baptism is not a false sign."[29] The sign remains with us throughout life and penance can only return us to it.

An important insight in Luther is relating our union to Christ in baptism to our priesthood as believers. Baptism into Christ makes us all priests: "For whoever comes out of the water of baptism can boast that he is already a consecrated priest, bishop, and pope. . . . We are all priests of equal standing."[30] Though the work we have to do may differ, all Christians have been made priests through their union with Christ's priesthood. In 1520, Luther is proclaiming a radical equality on the basis of baptism, overturning all ecclesiastical status. This is as radical as he gets.

Zwingli's interests do not lend themselves to much emphasis on union to Christ through baptism. In his concern to link the baptism of John to that of Christ, he misses the radically new dimension of baptism into Christ. He does note in passing that immersion signifies death and reemergence signifies resurrection but as a pledge or sign. Rather than language of union, Zwingli speaks of our being "made like unto him."[31]

His Anabaptist opponents saw baptism clearly as uniting them to Christ, especially in his suffering. The Schleitheim Confession indicates that baptism is for "all those who desire to walk in the resurrection of Jesus Christ and be buried with him in death, so that they might rise with him."[32] These were all-too-present realities since so many of the early Anabaptist leaders were martyred. Christ's equation of his baptism and his death was often their own experience. Hans Hut speaks of a baptism of blood that "Christ shows his disciples when he says that they are to be baptized with the baptism which witnesses to the whole world when a disciple's blood is spilt."[33] It was easy to turn this metaphor into an image against infant baptism. Dirk Philips argued that "those who are marked by this sign confess that one is baptized in Christ Jesus and into his death in order to be buried, and rise to a new life with him."[34] Children cannot perceive this; therefore, their baptism is nonsense.

Calvin by no means shies away from the image of our union to Christ. He speaks of our being "engrafted in Christ" and says again "that through baptism Christ makes us sharers in his death, that we may be engrafted in it." In baptism, we are "so united to Christ himself that we become sharers in all his blessings."[35] Calvin turns the Anabaptist argument around and argues that infants do indeed participate in Christ's death. God is good to children as well as to adults, and they receive all his benefits. The offspring of believers are also under the care of God, who acknowledges them as children of God.

In the past, the Anglican and Methodist traditions do not seem to have placed much emphasis on our union with Christ's death and resurrection either in creedal statements or in liturgical texts. The Westminster Confession lists "ingrafting into Christ" as one of the effects of baptism.[36] *A Directory for the Publique Worship of God*, 1645 (also called the *Westminster Directory*), uses another biological metaphor, praying "that the Child may be planted into the likeness of the death and resurrection of Christ."[37]

Once again, those traditions that resumed adult immersion, beginning in the seventeenth century, have often seen in this process an image of death and burial with Christ. The image of cleansing may be in the forefront, but death and burial is not far behind. Indeed, a facetious answer to the question "How much water is necessary for baptism?" has been given: "Enough to die in."[38] The symbolism of going down into a watery grave and rising again is obvious. One speaks of baptism as both womb and tomb, combining the metaphors of new birth and union to Christ.

Today, the metaphor of union with Christ's death and resurrection is experiencing a widespread revival in popularity. This is part of a much wider revival of the paschal sense of all Christian worship. This is shown in the renewed emphasis on the paschal nature of Sunday, the dominance of the Easter cycle, and linking of baptism to the Easter vigil. It is significant that *Baptism, Eucharist and Ministry* lists "Participation in Christ's Death and Resurrection" first under "The Meaning of Baptism." It speaks of identification with the death of Christ and burial and resurrection with him in liberation from slavery to sin.

It should not surprise us that similar sentiments appear in many new baptismal rites. The United Methodist rite speaks of Jesus as calling "his disciples / to share in the baptism of his death and resurrection" and prays for those now baptized that, "dying and being raised with Christ, / *they* may share in his final victory."[39] The Easter Vigil provides for baptisms, or reaffirmations of baptism. In the Episcopal Church, the Great Vigil of Easter also includes baptisms on this occasion plus the renewal by all of baptismal vows. The baptismal rite is explicit: "In it [the water of Baptism] we are buried with Christ in his death. By it we share in his resurrection."[40] Fleeting mention is made in the Lutheran rite of Christ's "baptism of his own death and resurrection."[41] The Minister's Desk Edition of the *Lutheran Book of Worship* provides for baptisms or renewals at the Easter Vigil. The Presbyterian Great Vigil of Easter encourages baptisms or reaffirmation of the baptismal covenant. The baptismal rite makes specific reference to Romans 6:3-5: "In it [the water of baptism] we are buried with Christ in his death. / From it we are raised to share in his resurrection."[42] It would be premature to say that Easter vigils are common among Protestants, but the texts are available today as never before.

The sense of union to Christ's priestly ministry as well as to his death and resurrection has also had an important impact on new understandings of the role of the laity in the ministry of the church. We shall return to this.

INCORPORATION INTO THE CHURCH

Closely related to union to Christ is the sense of incorporation into his church. The classic text is Paul's statement that "We were all baptized into one body" (1 Cor. 12:13). This reappears in several instances, as where Paul states that for those "baptized into Christ . . . there is no longer Jew or Greek, there is no longer slave or free, there is no longer male and female; for all of you are one in Christ Jesus" (Gal. 3:27-28). Baptism is the sign-act of entrance into the church and hence fonts are often placed at doors to churches.

From the earliest times, baptism was seen as the means of becoming a part of the church. This is all the more graphic in the East where baptism immediately leads to reception of the eucharist. But this had lapsed in the West by the twelfth century. Where church and society were synonymous, as in Europe during the late Middle Ages, baptism lost much sense of being an entrance rite into the Christian community. Instead, the mother was often required to be "churched" or purified after giving birth.

Luther has so much to say about the personal dimension of baptism that the communal aspect is less apparent. He does argue that "infants are aided by the faith of others, namely, those who bring them for baptism."[43] Even in a long exposition of the meaning of baptism in the Large Catechism, 1529, Luther simply describes baptism as that "through which we are first received into the Christian community."[44] The rest deals with the personal benefits of baptism. In a sense, this may be another sign of Luther's conservatism, for the sense of reception into the Christian community was not a high priority for his contemporaries.

Not so with Zwingli, who builds much of his theology around baptism as a sign and seal of community. Ironically, he is replying to the Anabaptists, who also stressed baptism as entrance into the Christian community. Indeed, until the debates of 1525, it appeared that Zwingli might be persuaded to abandon infant baptism. In his first reply to the Anabaptists, *Of Baptism*, 1525, Zwingli made a clear connection between baptism and circumcision as a covenant sign. Baptism is a sign of identification with the Christian community and Zwingli speaks of it as "simply a mark or pledge by which those who receive it are dedicated to God."[45] As such, it is an outward sign of our incorporation into the covenant community of the church. It acts as a public proclamation or identification of the Christian before his or her neighbors. The suggestion of infant baptism as dedication, about which he does not elaborate, may be the first use of such a term. Others picked it up including the Anabaptist Pilgram Marpeck. But Anabaptists consistently denied Zwingli's connection of baptism with circumcision or any attempt to prove infant baptism from the household accounts in Acts.

For Anabaptists, baptism was a clear sign of entrance into the pure and undefiled church. In Hubmaier's baptismal rite, the bishop lays hands on the newly baptized and declares: "I testify to you and give you authority that henceforth you shall be counted among the Christian community, as a member participating in the use of her keys, breaking bread and praying with other Christian sisters and brothers."[46] Of course, they could also be excluded by the ban. Baptism thus becomes the barrier between the pure church and the world.

Hans Denck could speak of baptism as "enrollment in the fellowship of believers."[47] For Pilgram Marpeck, only those who had died to sin and risen in Christ may be baptized, and then "having put on Jesus Christ, they will be accepted into the communion of Christ."[48] But it was left to Calvin to draw out the full implications of baptism as incorporation: "Baptism is for us a kind of entry into the church. For in it we have a testimony that we, while otherwise strangers and aliens, were received into the family of God, so that we are reckoned among his household."[49] Like Zwingli, Calvin acknowledges that baptism is "our confession before men."[50] Baptism is most appropriate for the children of believers: "Because by the blessing of the promise they already belonged to the body of Christ, they are received into the church with this solemn sign."[51] There is, then, a corporate nature of faith that children share with their parents. Circumcision foreshadows baptism; both place children within the company of the elect. The covenant made with children of believers includes them already in their mother's womb.

Baptism is not absolutely necessary to salvation but to neglect it through sloth is an affront to God. But the church is necessary: "For there is no other way to enter into life unless this mother [the church] conceive us in her womb, give us birth, nourish us at her breast, and lastly, . . . keep us under her care and guidance."[52] Calvin is here speaking of the visible church as the mother of believers. The true church is found wherever "the Word of God [is] purely preached and heard, and the sacraments administered according to Christ's institution."[53] Baptism is commanded of God and becomes the means through which we recognize ourselves as part of the church, which is necessary to salvation. None of the elect will die "before being sanctified and regenerated," and this implies being baptized.[54] Calvin has worked out the full ecclesiological consequences of baptism so that baptism places us in the only place where salvation is possible.

The Anglican Articles of Religion tell us that "they that receive Baptism rightly are grafted into the Church,"[55] but the Westminster Confession of Faith is even more specific in speaking of "the solemn admission of the party baptized into the visible Church."[56] For the

New England Puritans, it was crucial that the children of baptized Christians be admitted by baptism even though their parents could not own the covenant. Their English brethren thanked God that through baptism, God "daily brings some into the bosom of his Church" and the child is "solemnly entered into the household of faith."[57]

A curious anomaly developed in nineteenth-century American Methodism, where in 1864 a rite appeared for a "Form for Receiving Persons into the Church after Probation." This provided for adults already baptized who were now to "be received into full membership in the Church." The new members were admitted on the basis of "six months on trial."[58] In the early twentieth century, this shifted and children became "preparatory" members. Not until 1988 was this distinction eliminated in the baptismal rites and it made clear that all those baptized become "*members* of Christ's universal Church." They are also asked to "be loyal to The United Methodist Church."[59] As of 1998, the implications for United Methodist Church law are still unclear about how membership is defined. Any implication that baptism is not equivalent to membership in the church seems in conflict with scripture. For antipedobaptists, the question is not likely to arise since baptism of believers implies full admission into the church. It is also characteristic that almost all Protestant groups insist that baptism be a public act in front of the congregation.

With the heightened ecclesiological consciousness in Protestant churches in recent decades, it is not surprising that incorporation has received much attention. Baptism has become an ecumenical rallying point because most Christians accept the validity of other communions' baptisms. *Baptism, Eucharist and Ministry* makes "Incorporation into the Body of Christ" a major component of baptismal meaning and sees "our common baptism . . . [as] a basic bond of unity."[60] Baptism is a clear call to end divisions.

These theological shifts are apparent in recent rites. The United Methodist rite begins by affirming that through baptism "we are initiated into Christ's holy Church"[61] and ends with welcome into "the body of Christ / and in this congregation / of the United Methodist Church." A rubric specifies that "it is most fitting that the service continue with Holy Communion, in which the union of the new members with the body of Christ is most fully expressed. The new members, including children, may receive first."[62] It is characteristic of most

Protestant rites that they refer to membership in a local congregation as well as the universal church.

The Episcopal Church prays that "we bring into his [Christ's] fellowship those who have come to him in faith" and after baptism welcomes them, declaring, "we receive you into the household of God."[63] The Lutheran rite speaks of being "made members of the Church which is the body of Christ."[64] The newly baptized are welcomed "into the Lord's family . . . as fellow members of the body of Christ, children of the same heavenly Father."[65] Presbyterians proclaim that "by water and the Holy Spirit, / we are made members of the church, the body of Christ."[66] They are the most emphatic, declaring after baptism that "N. and N. have been received into the one holy catholic and apostolic church through baptism. / God has made *them members* of the household of God, / to share with us in the priesthood of Christ."[67]

It should not be overlooked that all but the Lutheran rite deliberately speak of "the baptismal covenant." The Lutheran revisers rejected covenant language as too Reformed. Yet the covenant is an Old Testament image of the people of God now newly back in style. The Presbyterian rite says:

> Through baptism we enter the covenant God has established.
> Within this covenant God gives us new life,
> guards us from evil,
> and nurtures us in love.
> In embracing that covenant, we choose whom we will serve,
> by turning from evil
> and turning to Jesus Christ.[68]

In language reminiscent of Joshua 24, the image of a covenant people is recycled in the context of the church. This is a relatively new development in baptismal rites, yet it has ancient roots.

RECEPTION OF THE HOLY SPIRIT

Closely related to incorporation into the church is the metaphor of reception of the Holy Spirit in baptism since the church is often seen as the environment of the Spirit's activity. The *Apostolic Tradition* has a recurring doxology, "in the Holy Spirit and the holy Church," which has recently been adopted by some churches. Jesus' own baptism has a theophany of the Holy Spirit visible as a dove (Matt. 3:16). Acts 2:38 says "be baptized . . . and you will receive the gift of the Holy Spirit." However, the connection is complicated by other passages in Acts such as 10:47, where the Holy Spirit arrives before baptism, or 19:6, where it arrives afterward with the laying on of hands. Other images refer to the Holy Spirit's activity in initiation as illumination or enlightenment (Heb. 6:4), or sanctification (1 Cor. 6:11).

Many sign-acts such as giving salt or a lighted candle as emblems of wisdom underscore the connection of the Holy Spirit with baptism. Representations of the baptism of Jesus with the dove representing the Holy Spirit have a long history. But before the Reformation, the work of the Holy Spirit in baptism in the West had become almost as ignored as it was in the eucharist.

The work of the Holy Spirit is not prominent in Luther's baptismal piety. This is simply another sign of his basic conservatism. The unclean spirit being exorcised gets almost as much attention in his baptismal rites as does the Holy Spirit. Zwingli distinguishes between an internal baptism of the Spirit, which is trust in Christ and is necessary, and the external baptism of the Spirit, such as speaking in tongues, which is unnecessary.[69] Water baptism is not intrinsically related to either and the Holy Spirit seems marginal in the whole process of initiation.[70]

But it was far from marginal to the Anabaptists. For them, it was the Holy Spirit that moved people to request baptism in water. The theme of three baptisms—"the Spirit and the water and the blood"—appears frequently in the Anabaptists' writings, based on a favorite text, 1 John 5:6-8. Hubmaier declares that the baptism of the Spirit "is an inner illumination of our hearts that takes place by the Holy Spirit, through the living Word of God."[71] He relates it to John 3:5, "of water and Spirit." By the Spirit, a convert is prompted to repent and turn to faith and seek, subsequently, water baptism, which may lead to tribulation and suffering.

According to Hans Hut, the Spirit is the first part of baptism, "the assurance in and surrender to the divine Word that a man will live according to what the Word proclaims."[72]

One would expect Calvin to have more to say about the Holy Spirit in baptism, in light of his theology of the eucharist. He does allude to the fact that elect children, dying after baptism, are renewed by the

Lord "by the power, incomprehensible to us, of his Spirit, in whatever way he alone foresees will be expedient."[73] A back-handed affirmation of the Spirit in baptism occurs in his deploring confirmation as "an overt outrage against baptism" in implying that the Holy Spirit still needs to be received by laying on of hands.[74]

The English prayer book of 1549 speaks of being "baptized by the holy ghost," and 1552 corrects it to "with water and the holy ghost." The 1549 book speaks of the newly baptized as having been regenerated "by water and the holy ghost." The "holy spirit" is invoked in the monthly rite of blessing the font water in 1549;[75] this disappears in 1552. But the image of the Holy Spirit is well present in the rites and is expanded in 1662 with prayer to "sanctify *him* with the holy Ghost." Wesley kept this prayer, and it was in the Methodist rites until 1916, when the entire prayer over the font was dropped by the Methodist Episcopal Church.

The Holy Spirit is full of surprises and shows up where one might least expect. Robert Barclay was the great Quaker theologian. Barclay claims that water baptism "was commanded for a time, and not to continue for ever."[76] He argues that Quakers do have a baptism of the Spirit and fire but that it is an inward washing and purging from sins. The gospel ends carnal ordinances but not spiritual ones, and Spirit-filled worship is the Quaker equivalent of baptism.

In the twentieth century, various American Pentecostal churches built differing theologies of baptism in the Spirit and gifts of the Spirit. Much of this derived from nineteenth-century holiness movements that focused on the second blessing or entire sanctification as gifts of the Holy Spirit following justification. Most Pentecostal churches continue water baptism, many of them including infants. But baptism of the Spirit seems to be detached from water baptism and much more important. Frequently it is made manifest by various gifts of the Spirit, such as healing, prophesying, interpretation, and speaking in tongues. Since 1960, many of these gifts have become manifest among mainline Protestants and Roman Catholics.

A minor controversy occurred in the Church of England in the 1940s when Gregory Dix, O.S.B., insisted on the importance of confirmation as the primary giving of the Holy Spirit.[77] His opponents claimed he was splitting the Holy Spirit,[78] and Dix's views on this subject are shared by few today.

But this metaphor does reappear in our own time. *Baptism, Eucharist*

and Ministry speaks of "The Gift of the Spirit" as an essential meaning: "God bestows upon all baptized persons the anointing and the
promise of the Holy Spirit, marks them with a seal and implants in
their hearts the first installment of their inheritance as sons and
daughters of God."[79] Nor should we be surprised that the images of
water and Spirit are especially abundant in new baptismal rites. The
United Methodist rite has restored, after an absence of sixty years, the
thanksgiving over the water. It invokes God to "pour out your Holy
Spirit, / to bless this gift of water and *those* who *receive* it." Hands are
laid on the newly baptized immediately with the words "The Holy
Spirit work within you, / that being born through water and the Spirit,
you may be a faithful disciple of Jesus Christ."[80]

The Episcopal rite, again, invites God to sanctify the water "by the
power of your Holy Spirit." A prayer asks, "Sustain them, O Lord, in
your Holy Spirit," and the laying on of hands is done with the words
"*N.* you are sealed by the Holy Spirit in Baptism and marked as
Christ's own for ever."[81] The Lutheran rite invites, "Pour out your
Holy Spirit, so that *those* who *are* baptized may be given new life."[82]
After baptism, the sevenfold gifts of the Spirit are invoked. In the
Presbyterian rite, God is invoked: "Send your Spirit to move over this
water / that it may be a fountain of deliverance and rebirth."[83] After
baptism, the laying on of hands is accompanied by the words "O Lord,
uphold N. by your Holy Spirit," and the sevenfold gifts cited.[84] The
sign of the cross may be given with oil (optional) with the words "N.
child of the covenant, / you have been sealed by the Holy Spirit in
baptism, / and marked as Christ's own forever."[85] There is little doubt
that the metaphor of the reception of the Holy Spirit has come into its
own in recent liturgical revision after long centuries of neglect.

NEW BIRTH OR REGENERATION

In some ways, the metaphor of new birth or regeneration has been
the most controversial of all. It overlaps union to Christ and incorporation into the church. The classic text is Johannine: "No one can enter
the kingdom of God without being born of water and Spirit" (John
3:5). The word *paliggenesías*, literally "again born," appears in Titus 3:5:
"He saved us . . . through the water of rebirth and the renewal by the
Holy Spirit." This language brings to mind aspects of our experience

of God's grace that correspond to women's role as bearers of children. Some fonts have been designed to suggest a pregnant woman.

Medieval rites for blessing the font utilized the metaphor of the font as the womb of the church. This complemented the tomb imagery of death and resurrection. And the John 3:5 passage helped solidify the teaching of the necessity of baptism for salvation. The Council of Trent simply reiterated that baptism is "necessary unto salvation." Luther is reluctant to put much emphasis on new birth. He does quote Titus 3:5 in the Small Catechism and cites the same reference in the Large Catechism. Zwingli seems even less fond of birth imagery, possibly because it certainly implies that baptism effects a change and he shuns anything causative. Among the Anabaptists, baptism could be a sign of rebirth, not a cause. Peter Riedeman writes that when one has heard and believed the Word, "whosoever is born in this wise, to him belongs baptism as a bath of re-birth, signifying that he has entered into the covenant of the grace and knowledge of God."[86] Baptism is more a sign that rebirth has already occurred than a factor in causing it. Calvin, too, is reluctant to use birth imagery, partly because he does not want to make baptism necessary for salvation as Lutheran and Roman Catholic confessions did. He does ever so briefly mention that "believers are reborn into newness of life and into the fellowship of Christ."[87] But only the elect experience regeneration, and many experience it before birth while in the womb. John the Baptist himself is cited as an example (Luke 1:15).[88] Elsewhere, Calvin interprets John 3:5 by saying, "I simply understand 'water and Spirit' as 'Spirit, who is water.'"[89] Calvin is more concerned about what the Spirit does to regenerate the elect than about stressing the unity of water and rebirth.

On the other hand, the Anglican rite of 1549 is full of allusions to John 3:5: no one "can enter into the kingdom of God (except he be regenerate, and born anew of water, and the holy ghost)"; "this wholesome laver of regeneration"; "by spiritual regeneration"; "they may be born again"; "who hath regenerate thee by water and the holy ghost."[90] The Articles of Religion speak of baptism as "a sign of Regeneration or New-Birth." John Wesley kept this part of the article on baptism. But he did have difficulty in envisioning regeneration as assured in all cases, particularly adults. Consequently, his rite for infant baptism kept some of the phrases above, which had been around for two centuries, but he was reluctant to presume that all adults baptized were truly regenerate. Wesley had come to see new birth in terms of a conscious conversion experience. This meant for him that baptismal regeneration could not be presumed past childhood. And so becoming a Christian involved a born-again experience that was not marked by external ceremony or rite but was a life-transforming personal experience.

This concept of the born-again Christian became a staple of American revivalism and the Frontier Tradition and is very much present in American religion today. Many evangelicals do not regard undergoing baptism, particularly infant baptism, as being born again. The new birth they see as a conscious conversion experience, often followed by baptism. Some churches now provide rites of baptismal renewal, affirmation, or reaffirmation for those who have a major conversion experience after baptism.

In the Church of England, a major controversy arose in 1847 when a priest by the name of G. C. Gorham in the diocese of Exeter refused to believe that baptism caused regeneration and that Article XXVII, "Of Baptism," merely said it was "a sign of Regeneration or New-Birth." His bishop, Henry Phillpotts, was a high churchman who wanted to insist that baptism effected what it signified.[91] It posed a divergence of opinions between most Anglican evangelicals, who insisted on baptism as only a sign, and high church types, who had a causative view of the sacrament. This division is hardly resolved even today.

The metaphor of new birth has received more attention in recent years, partly because it is the most explicitly feminine metaphor the church has. *Baptism, Eucharist and Ministry* neglects it partly because some groups identify new birth with conversion, not baptism. The United Methodist rite speaks of being "given new birth through water and the Spirit" and mentions "Jesus, nurtured in the water of a womb," and "being born through water and the Spirit."[92] The Episcopal rite speaks of being "reborn by the Holy Spirit," being "cleansed from sin and born again."[93] For Lutherans, "in the waters of Baptism we are reborn children of God."[94] Presbyterians pray "that this font may be your womb of new birth."[95] So the metaphor of new birth is in the process of being rediscovered. As one of the most explicitly feminine images in all of scripture, it can help balance overwhelmingly masculine imagery.

BAPTISM AND SOCIAL JUSTICE

As we have just seen, baptism has a wide impact on life within the churches and beyond. We are gradually becoming more aware of just how dynamic its impact is on issues of social justice.[96]

In the first place, baptism conveys a sense of absolute equality. Tertullian, in arguing for the possibility of lay administration of baptism, said, "That which is received on equal terms can be given on equal terms."[97] Throughout history, laypeople have administered baptism, although the Reformers were very clerical in reserving baptism to clergy. This is especially true of Calvin and Wesley. Luther, of course, made the connection between baptism and the priesthood of all believers. The Lutheran rite ends by declaring, "Through Baptism God has made *these* new *sisters and brothers members* of the priesthood we all share in Christ Jesus."[98]

Baptism, then, is the basis of Christian democracy and as such, our most fertile soil for ecumenism. All Christians come forth from the waters of baptism in the same spiritual condition. As Paul insisted, in baptism there are no Jews nor Greeks nor slaves nor free nor male nor female. And, we might add, no rich or poor, no communists or capitalists. Baptism forms a common base level. In the days of the civil rights movement, it was common to refer to baptism as the "sacrament of integration."

Baptism also engenders a profound sense of responsibility for our fellow members of the household of faith. It is a contradiction of our baptism that we should have so many homeless and poor in our society, many of whom are baptized into us. We undertake in baptism a serious responsibility not only for the spiritual welfare but also the material welfare of our fellow members of the body of Christ. The two cannot be separated. The deprivation of our neighbor is a sign of our failure to take our baptism seriously. On the other hand, deeds of love and charity are a form of living out our baptism.

Most of the new baptismal rites have strong statements of renunciation of evil. Methodists pledge "to resist evil, injustice, and oppression / in whatever forms they present themselves."[99] Episcopalians reject "Satan and all the spiritual forces of wickedness . . . [and] the evil powers of this world."[100] Presbyterians are called to "renounce evil and its power in the world."[101] These renunciations are written specifically to stress the nature of sin as social and not just private temptation.

71

How much they are taken seriously can be questioned, but at least congregations and those they baptize are being confronted with these questions.

The Anabaptists were very much aware of the threat that baptism meant for them, since it often led to martyrdom. The message of water baptism was clear: it led to baptism of blood. The message of baptism today calls also for sacrifice and surrender. Fortunately there are in every generation those who realize what a radical demand baptism places on the church to be involved in struggles for social justice. It is indeed the gospel in water.

CHAPTER FOUR

The Eucharist in Practice and Controversy

The Reformation brought great changes in eucharistic practice and faith. The most important change was the one least expected, that is, the shift from the eucharist being the central act of Christian worship to being an occasional service. Most of the Reformers never desired such a momentous change; many of them wanted a weekly eucharist. But for a variety of reasons, largely beyond their control, the eucharist was often replaced in its central role and became marginal. It came to be celebrated at monthly, quarterly, or even yearly intervals.

Most changes in practice were the result of controversies or produced controversies in their wake. It is important to trace the most significant changes in practice and the controversies associated with them. We cannot touch on all the shifts involved but shall focus on such central issues as the experience of the presence of Christ, frequency, presiders, communicants' participation, and the communion elements themselves. The next chapter will explore what these changes have meant to people at various times and places.

THE EUCHARISTIC HERITAGE

Medieval Christianity had made the eucharist the central act of worship for the laity outside religious communities. By the late

Middle Ages, some laity might attend Sunday vespers and there were the occasional baptisms, weddings, and funerals. But the eucharist constituted the normal worship for the laity on Sundays and feast days and was celebrated daily by priests. By this time, it had acquired a highly numinous quality focusing on the presence of Christ in the consecrated elements.

In terms of piety, this meant a focus on seeing Christ visibly present in the bread after consecration. Participation meant basically seeing the host, what is known as ocular communion. Thus the high point of the mass was not receiving communion as food but feeding the eyes through the gaze that saves. The elevation was the high point, heralded by the ringing of bells. Some people raced from church to church to observe this climax at several churches on a Sunday morning.[1] Christ was physically and visibly present for all present to behold.

Since the mass was entirely in Latin and key portions of it said in a low voice, hearing was not an important experience of Christ's presence. In 1547, an English bishop, Stephen Gardiner, wrote:

> For in times past, . . . the people in church took small heed what the priest and the clerks did in the chancel, but only to stand up at the Gospel and kneel at the Sacring [bell], or else every man was occupied him self severally [individually] in several prayer. . . . And therefore it was never meant that the people should indeed hear the Matins or hear the Mass, but be present there and pray themselves in silence.[2]

The congregation was occupied in private prayer while the priest celebrated mass on their behalf. What they were doing was basically devotional rather than liturgical.

Preaching was sporadic and not considered an essential part of the mass. Various religious orders had sprung up in an attempt to remedy this lack and some hall-type churches were built to make preaching more feasible. Much preaching by itinerant preachers occurred at the market cross instead of at mass. The linkage of Word and altar was vague at best.

People received communion rarely, often only once a year at Easter. Zurich, where it was common to receive communion four times a year, was the exception, not the rule. Ever since the Fourth Lateran Council of 1215, it had been mandated that confession should precede communion and this had contributed to a generally penitential approach to the eucharist. Lent became the time for one's annual confession in preparation for Easter communion. But any time was appropriate for adoration of the reserved sacrament in a pyx, aumbry, or sacrament house.

The presence of Christ in the consecrated bread and wine had been the source of theological reflection from the ninth century onward. By the thirteenth century, a new term had come into vogue, the word *transubstantiation*. Using philosophical categories derived from Aristotle, a rationalistic approach was developed in order to define how the church experiences Christ's presence in the eucharist. The result was a distinction between substance, what is really present, and accidents, what the senses can detect. According to Aquinas, "the whole substance of the bread is changed into the whole substance of Christ's body, and the whole substance of the wine into the whole substance of Christ's blood." Aquinas denied that "the substance of bread and wine remains in this sacrament after consecration,"[3] although theologians continued to debate this point. Transubstantiation defines the radical change that occurs in the elements after their consecration. The doctrine represents the triumph of the desire to understand a miracle over the possibility of understanding the miraculous.

The mass was also looked at as a sacrifice through which the work of Christ was mediated to those present or those paying for the mass. This was based on the prevailing belief in the inability of humans to satisfy God's justice by their own efforts. Only Christ can make this restitution. As St. Anselm wrote in 1098: "What greater mercy could be imagined, than for God the Father to say to the sinner, . . . 'Receive my only-begotten Son' . . . ?"[4] The eucharist became the chief vehicle for appropriating this atoning work of Christ. Mass could be said to procure all kinds of benefits for oneself or one's friends and family. Abuses, such as seeking the death of an enemy, were repeatedly condemned by various councils and synods. But the mass was an integral part of the whole process of atonement between God and humans. It is no wonder that it played such a central role in medieval piety.

And it had a great impact on both the living and the dead. Eamon Duffy says "the influence of the cult of the dead was ubiquitous"[5] in late medieval piety, producing "an enormous inflation of the number of priestly ordinations in the later Middle Ages."[6] The living were urged to relieve the suffering of those in purgatory "by securing Masses for the repose of their souls."[7] The cult of the dead was crucial in financing thousands of priests who had no parochial responsibilities and income but earned a living by saying masses for the dead. The economic consequences of masses for the dead were enormous, all based on the mass as a means of appropriating Christ's saving work for oneself and for others.

THE DEBATES OVER HOW THE PRESENCE OF CHRIST IS EXPERIENCED

The central fact of the eucharist throughout history has been the Christian community's experience of the presence of Christ in it. But ever since the ninth century, the West had been embroiled in controversies over how best to express what the church experiences in the eucharist. Such controversies both reflected and shaped eucharistic practice and still continue to do so. So it is best to begin our investigation of eucharistic practices and controversies in Protestant churches with this central theme.

Luther's reaction to the official theology of transubstantiation as the best expression of the church's experience in the eucharist is drastic, even though his own theology is not that far distant in results. As late as 1519, in a sermon on the eucharist, he still seems to move within the framework of transubstantiation. But he does question reliance on it as simply *opus operatum*, done without any concern beyond the mere doing of it.[8] By October of 1520, he roundly condemns the doctrine of transubstantiation "as a figment of the human mind, for it rests neither on the Scriptures nor on reason." He does not deny the transformation of bread and wine into body and blood, but he rejects the idea that the substances of bread and wine disappear. His analogy, which may not be good physics, is that in red-hot iron "the two substances, fire and iron, are so mingled that every part is both iron and fire."[9]

It is a scandal that a pagan, Aristotle, could be used to define the central miracle of Christian worship. Philosophy cannot fathom a miracle that is clearly stated in the words of Christ in scripture. Only faith can perceive that both bread and body "remain there at the same time."[10] Christ is present in, with, and under bread and wine. This view, which had medieval precedents, avoids separating accidents from substance. It became Lutheran orthodoxy that "the true body and blood of Christ are really present in the Supper of our Lord under the form of bread and wine."[11]

If early on Luther found it necessary to resist philosophical attempts to define Christ's presence, he soon found it necessary to defend the eucharist from another form of rationalism. In 1521, the Dutch lawyer Cornelis Hoen wrote Luther to suggest that the "is" in "This is my body" really meant "signifies." Soon Andreas Carlstadt entered the fray and was joined by Oecolampadius and others, particularly Zwingli. While Luther was a literalist regarding "This is my body," Zwingli and others were literalists with "was taken up into heaven and sat down at the right hand of God" (Mark 16:19). For them, in his physical human nature, Christ was localized in heaven.

Luther was anything but subtle in his defense of the presence of Christ by both human and divine natures in the bread and wine. The title of one treatise, "That These Words of Christ, 'This Is My Body,' etc., Still Stand Firm Against the Fanatics," 1527, tells it all. It followed a shorter treatise from the year before in which Luther had argued for the clear and obvious meaning of the words of institution: "This is my body." He had claimed there that Christ "is present in all creatures, and I might find him in stone, in fire, in water, or even in a rope. . . . He is present everywhere, but he does not wish that you grope for him everywhere. Grope rather where the Word is."[12] This is the concept of the ubiquity of Christ by both divine and human natures. Thus Christ's body can be upon a thousand altars because the properties of one nature pertains to the other, the so-called *communicatio idiomatum*, a concept reaching back to the fifth century. In response to the charge that Luther confused the two natures, he accused Zwingli in 1528 "of separating the person of Christ as though there were two persons."[13] Luther denies that heaven is a place where Christ is confined and compares Zwingli's view of Christ in heaven to a stork's nest in a tree.

Zwingli, too, had received Hoen's letter and finally acted on it in 1524, agreeing in principle that "This is" means "This signifies." As Hoen had suggested, a wedding ring can be a sign to a widow of her husband. Whereas Luther clung to the institution narratives in the synoptics, Zwingli preferred John 6, in which Christ speaks of our eating his flesh and drinking his blood but ends by saying, "It is the spirit that gives life; the flesh is useless" (6:63). The crux of Zwingli's argument is that "This verb 'is,' then, is in my judgement used here for 'signifies,' " and John 6:63 is the proof.[14] It rings like a refrain through his writings.

All of this is in line with Zwingli's skepticism about outward signs. Christ is present in the eucharist but only in a spiritual and divine fashion, not identified with the communion elements. The sign and what it signifies are distinct. On the other hand, Zwingli believes Christ is present in the eucharist in His divine nature. In this sense, Zwingli demonstrates clearly that his view is based on a pre-Enlightenment worldview. His is still a sacral universe in which Christ can and does act. He hints that, by the Holy Spirit, God works in the eucharist. In the eucharist, we have a commemoration by which "all the benefits which God has displayed in his Son are called to mind. And by the signs themselves, the bread and wine, Christ himself is as it were set before our eyes."[15] Furthermore, when believers "feed spiritually upon Christ, . . . when you join with your brethren in partaking of the bread and wine which are the tokens of the body of Christ, then in the true sense of the word you eat him sacramentally."[16]

The inevitable conflict came to a head in 1529 when Luther met Zwingli and others in the castle at Marburg for a high-level summit meeting. Luther summed it all up by saying to Bucer (on Zwingli's side), "Our spirit is different from yours; it is clear that we do not possess the same spirit."[17] The upshot was that they agreed to disagree "as to whether the true body and blood of Christ are bodily present in the bread and wine."[18]

By and large, the Anabaptists felt comfortable within the parameters of Zwingli's description of the means of Christ's presence in the eucharist. As with Zwingli, much of the emphasis was on the community itself rather than on the elements. As Menno Simons writes, "by the Lord's Supper Christian unity, love, and peace are signified and enjoined." It is a memorial of "all the glorious fruits of divine love."[19]

John Calvin was essentially a second-generation reformer, and he could profit from all that preceded him. In this case, he deliberately set out to mediate between Luther and Zwingli. Calvin's friend Martin Bucer had moved since Marburg to a position closer to Luther. In restating how the church experiences the presence of Christ in the eucharist, Calvin gives us the most sophisticated expression of this experience among the Reformers. Essentially, Zwingli made too little of the signs, Luther and the Catholics too much. Like Zwingli, Calvin believes that Christ's humanity is located in heaven;[20] ubiquity he calls a "monstrous notion."[21] Yet, Calvin faults Zwingli for having "too little regard for the signs," thus divorcing "them from their mysteries."[22]

Without "extolling them immoderately," Calvin wants to give the signs full value as God's means of encounter with us:

> If the Lord truly represents the participation in his body through the breaking of bread, there ought not to be the least doubt that he truly presents and shows his body. . . . For why should the Lord put in your hand the symbol of his body, except to assure you of a true participation in it? . . . Let us no less surely trust that the body itself is also given to us.[23]

He repeats this many times: "We must then really receive in the Supper the body and blood of Jesus Christ. . . . The internal substance of the sacrament is joined with the visible signs."[24] Or again, "adding the reality to the symbol . . . he thus also makes us partakers of his substance."[25]

But Christ's human body is confined to heaven. Calvin asks in his Catechism of the Church in Geneva how we can be joined to Christ and replies: "He accomplishes this by the miraculous and secret virtue of his Spirit, for whom it is not difficult to associate things that are otherwise separated by an interval of space."[26] Calvin has picked up a mere hint of Zwingli and made the Holy Spirit a central actor in the eucharist. To use a modern analogy, the Holy Spirit operates like an escalator to raise us up to heaven where we truly feed on Christ. The rediscovery of the importance of the Holy Spirit in the eucharist, long forgotten in the West but central in the East, is an important accomplishment in Calvin. As he says, "a serious wrong is done to the Holy Spirit, unless we believe that it is through his incomprehensible power that we come to partake of Christ's flesh and blood. . . . The secret power of the Spirit is the bond of our union with Christ."[27]

Ultimately, Calvin recognizes that how this union occurs is a mystery which reason cannot contain. "I shall not be ashamed to confess that it is a secret too lofty for either my mind to comprehend or my words to declare. And, to speak more plainly, I rather experience than understand it."[28] Neither the scholastics nor Zwingli, the rationalists of the right and left, can grasp this mystery; all that is left to do is to experience the "true and substantial partaking of the body and blood of the Lord."[29] Unfortunately, this does not work for the wicked or unbelievers. Lutherans insisted on the objective reality of Christ's body and blood even for the wicked. Lutherans Joachim Westphal and Tileman Heshusius engaged with Calvin in long and bitter debate over communion of the impious. The result was a permanent division between Lutherans and the Reformed. Intercommunion, in North America, was not realized until as late as 1997.

In one of the most momentous decisions in the history of the eucharist, Thomas Cranmer, primate of the Church of England, chose to lean more on what Brian Gerrish calls Zwingli's "symbolic memorialism" or the "symbolic parallelism" of Zwingli's successor Heinrich Bullinger than on Calvin's "symbolic instrumentalism."[30] Of the three, Cranmer's view most approaches that of Bullinger, that the sign refers to a "happening that occurs simultaneously in the present."[31] In Cranmer's final liturgical text of 1552, the influence of Zwingli seems strong, yet Cranmer did resist the "black rubric" that insisted no adoration was meant to the elements by kneeling. Martin Bucer pleaded with Cranmer to keep the words "may worthily receive the most precious body and blood of thy son Jesus Christ," but they disappeared when the prayer was deconstructed in 1552, although similar words did remain in the "Prayer of Humble Access." More telling still, the words of administration shift from 1549's "The body of our Lord Jesus Christ which was given for thee, preserve thy body and soul unto everlasting life" to "Take and eat this, in remembrance that Christ died for thee, and feed on him in thy heart by faith, with thanksgiving" in 1552.[32] With a touch that was both theologically and politically astute, Queen Elizabeth I reunited these two phrases in the 1559 prayer book. Cranmer also seemed to place a higher value on the eucharist than Zwingli by continuing its weekly celebration.

The Scots Confession of 1560 condemned those who considered the sacraments as "nothing else but naked and bare signs" and insisted that the Holy Ghost "carries us above all things that are visible, carnal, and earthly, and makes us to feed upon the body and blood of *Christ Jesus*" so that we are "made flesh of his flesh, and bone of his bones."[33] This sounds like pure Calvinism. And it is echoed almost a century later in the *Westminster Directory* of 1645, which directs prayer "that we may receive by faith the Body and Blood of Jesus Christ crucified for us, and so to feed upon him, that he may be one with us, and we with him."[34]

But a gradual drift toward a more memorialist direction seemed to pervade most branches of English Christianity throughout the seventeenth and eighteenth centuries. Another form of the black rubric against "idolatry" was reinstituted in the 1662 prayer book. On the other hand, there was a series of notable Anglicans who edged toward a more Catholic understanding, except that the word *transubstantiation* was an absolute taboo, as dictated by the Articles of Religion. Bishops Andrewes, Laud, Taylor, and others spoke in terms of a real presence. The opposite position was taken by Bishop Benjamin Hoadly in 1735. He argued that the phrase "in remembrance of me . . . implies his Bodily Absence" so that Christ is present only by memory.[35] The outcry against his book *A Plain Account* showed that the real absence was too radical for most Anglicans (or Zwingli, for that matter).

But the Enlightenment relished this idea of making sacraments solely a backward look to biblical times. To the worldview of the Enlightenment, anything that smacked of the supernatural was highly suspect. Zwingli's concept of the presence of Christ by his divine nature in the assembly was too supernatural for the desacralized mind of the Enlightenment. Biblical literalism and the Enlightenment made good companions because they both preferred to relegate divine activity to the first century.

Yet in the midst of this worldview, the Wesley brothers took a strong stand for the supernatural character of the eucharist as a means of grace. Taking their cue from Daniel Brevint, dean of Lincoln Cathedral in the previous century, they wrote what is still the greatest collection of eucharistic hymns in the English language, *Hymns on the Lord's Supper.* Published in 1745, it contains 166 hymns and is the best index of the Wesleys' experience of the eucharist.

In a number of ways, there are echoes of Calvin on eucharistic presence though the Wesleys sometimes dissociate themselves deliberately in such lines as "We need not now go up to heaven, / To bring the long-sought Saviour down"[36] or in the sections on sacrifice. But there is a strong instrumentalist theme, as of "an instrument ordain'd,"[37] in many of the hymns:

> Who shall say how bread and wine
> God into man conveys!
> *How* the bread His flesh imparts,

> *How* the wine transmits His blood,
> Fills His faithful people's hearts
> With all the life of God![38]

Elsewhere they ask God to "realize the sign." Like Calvin, they see the Holy Spirit as effecting the sacrament. And like Calvin, they feel that how the eucharist works remains a mystery, so that even angels "search it out in vain." Over and over, the Wesleys speak of "this mysterious bread" or "mysterious Supper." One wonders what might have been the course of Anglican liturgy if Cranmer had been more attuned to Calvin than to Zwingli and Bullinger. The Wesleys often also express a sense of the eucharist as a "converting ordinance" in which the presence of Christ moves one to deeper faith.

Recent research has shown that much of this stress on the presence of Christ in the eucharist pervaded early American Methodism.[39] Participation in the eucharist was usually limited to those in the Methodist societies and all others excluded. But, for the insiders, it could be an ecstatic encounter with the risen Savior, the presence of the king in the camp. A fervent eucharistic piety lasted longer in American Methodism than we once believed. The eucharist also came to be the climax of the frontier camp meeting where the newly converted joined those already saved at the Lord's table.

The current in much of American Protestantism was toward a memorial approach rather than present encounter. In a sense, the Enlightenment had conquered even the liturgically conservative Lutherans and spread as far left as the Unitarians. It is significant that when John Nevin wrote *The Mystical Presence: A Vindication of the Reformed or Calvinistic Doctrine of the Holy Eucharist* in 1846, he was simply rediscovering Calvin's eucharistic doctrine in contrast to what he calls "the modern Puritan theory" that was pervading all branches of American Protestantism. "Even in the Episcopal Church," he says, "few are willing to receive in full such representation of the eucharistic presence, as are made either by Hooker or Calvin."[40] But Nevin's efforts were shouted down by the prevailing Presbyterian guardian of orthodoxy, Charles Hodge of Princeton, whose views on the eucharist had a decidedly Zwinglian cast, albeit one filtered through an Enlightenment mentality.

But change was already underway in the Oxford Movement or Catholic Revival in the Church of England. There was a definite return to the concept of the real presence in the eucharist. Proponents could cite both writers of the early church and seventeenth-century bishops for the belief that Christ was effectively present in the bread and wine. This new emphasis led to the recovery of many practices lapsed since the Reformation, such as the sacrament being reserved in churches. More visibly, the Cambridge Movement led to a wholesale return to Gothic church architecture with remote but splendid high altars, vestments, and the full panoply of medieval ceremonial.[41] This in turn repelled many English and American Protestants who feared a return to Roman Catholic ways.

Yet Lutherans in places such as Neuendettelsau, Germany (Wilhelm Loehe), and Denmark (N. F. S. Grundtvig) began a return to the practices and theology of Luther. As with Nevin and Calvin, the cry was a return to the eucharistic doctrine of the reformers, especially concerning the presence of Christ. Yet, for most Lutherans as well as other Protestants, the eucharist functioned more as a memorial of Christ's past works than as present encounter with him. More altar-tables bore the words "In remembrance of me" than "Holy, Holy, Holy."

In the twentieth century, an exception must be made for the Pentecostals, who were not the least embarrassed by the sense of Christ's presence in their assemblies. Indeed, they relished the immediacy of the Spirit's presence as evidenced by various gifts such as healing, interpretation, and speaking in tongues. Among some Pentecostals, especially in England, the eucharist, however abbreviated, became an invariable part of Sunday worship. They had moved to a post-Enlightenment view in which the presence of Christ through the Holy Spirit was a basic given of all worship. It may be that the Spirit-filled gifts upstaged the eucharist at times, but there was no reluctance to sense Christ as present in the present tense rather than simply being memorialized in the past tense. The Spirit makes Christ present in all worship, eucharistic and noneucharistic.

This immediacy with Christ was not expressed in the mainline churches. Methodists got very nervous about words which had survived virtually intact since Cranmer in the "Prayer of Humble Access": "so to eat the flesh of thy Son Jesus Christ, and to drink his blood," and in the eucharistic prayer, "may be partakers of his most blessed body and blood." In 1939 these became "so to partake of these memorials of Thy Son Jesus Christ" and "may also be partakers of the divine nature through Him."[42] In the 1965 revision, the first of these was again altered to "so to partake of this Sacrament of thy Son Jesus Christ."[43]

Certainly this was as far as most Methodists were willing to go as late as 1965. Most Protestants had a memorialistic view of the sacrament then and probably do today. Even many Roman Catholics were not exempt. It is a significant shift that the 1989 United Methodist rite has shed its embarrassment about the real presence of Christ in the "gifts of bread and wine." It invokes the Holy Spirit:

> Make them be for us the body and blood of Christ,
> that we may be for the world the body of Christ,
> redeemed by his blood.[44]

Here is a deliberate return to language that John Wesley would have relished, although he did not see fit to change this prayer in his 1784 service book. And it is close to Cranmer's 1549 language "that they may be unto us the body and blood of thy most dearly beloved son Jesus Christ," words transmuted in 1552 into "may be partakers of his most blessed body and blood."[45]

Similar shifts are apparent in other new service books. The Episcopal Church now has a variety of eucharistic prayers, but typical is "Sanctify them by your Holy Spirit to be for your people the Body and Blood of your Son, the holy food and drink of new and unending life in him."[46] Some Lutherans have had difficulty in accepting a eucharistic prayer, although the words of institution are about as strong a statement of real presence as one could wish. One new prayer reads, "We who receive / the Lord's body and blood."[47] The Presbyterian language asks that the bread and cup "may be the communion of the body and blood of Christ." One alternative follows the Methodist wording. Another speaks of "showing them to be . . . the body and blood of your Son Jesus Christ."[48] Here is a sense of finally catching up to Calvin. Even more striking are the words of administration of the bread and cup: "The body of Christ, given for you. / The blood of Christ, given for you." (Methodist); "The Body of Christ, the bread of heaven. / The Blood of Christ, the cup of salvation." (Episcopal); or "The body of Christ, given for you. / The blood of Christ, shed for you." (Lutheran and Presbyterian). A similar trend is the gradual recovery of Wesley's eucharistic hymns among Methodists and the widely used recent hymns by Brian Wren and Fred Pratt Green. At last, it is possible to speak of Christ as giving himself to us as bread and wine.

THE FREQUENCY OF THE EUCHARIST

The most important change from the late medieval church was also the least expected or desired for most of the reformers. This was the marginalizing of the eucharist from the invariable Sunday service to an occasional service on monthly, quarterly, or annual cycles. Zwingli and most of the Anabaptists would not have been shocked at this development; most of their fellow reformers would have been.

In the late medieval church in the West, the eucharist was celebrated in most parish churches on a daily basis but attended by the whole village on Sundays and feast days (which were numerous). Yet communion was infrequent. The Council of Trent encouraged frequent communion but presumed it to be yearly, requiring those of sufficient age "to communicate every year, at least at Easter."[49] The sacrament was also reserved in the church for adoration and taken to the sick.

It probably never occurred to Luther that anything else would take the place of the eucharist for Sunday worship. His two Sunday services are both for the eucharist. A major change was that it now would always be accompanied by preaching of the Word. In 1523, he wrote: "A Christian congregation should never gather together without the preaching of God's Word and prayer."[50] At the same time, he said, "the daily masses should be completely discontinued,"[51] apparently because they rarely included a sermon.

What Luther expected remained in practice at least two centuries later in such cities as Leipzig, where Sunday "always included a celebration of the Holy Communion"[52] which might last four hours because of the large number of communicants. This was in addition to daily services of preaching and prayer. By the end of the eighteenth century, the weekly eucharist had disappeared in Leipzig, largely a victim of the Enlightenment. It was still common to have a weekly eucharist in Lutheran Sweden but this slowly eroded during the nineteenth century.[53] For American Lutherans, except the Swedes, the eucharist was an occasional service until recently.

In Zwingli's Zurich, the devout tended to receive communion more often than in many cities. In this case, it was common at the great festivals of Christmas, Easter, Pentecost, and the local patronal festival of Sts. Felix and Regula (September 11). This roughly quarterly arrangement suited Zwingli well, and beginning at Easter 1525 he provided for four yearly celebrations of the eucharist on these occasions.[54] In a sense, he was deeply conservative, eliminating the eucharists at which only the priest communed and retaining the communions to which the laity were accustomed: in other words, no communion, no eucharist.

By and large, the Anabaptists were content with occasional celebrations, especially since they often worshiped under perilous circumstances. Not so John Calvin. But he did not succeed in what he wanted, a weekly eucharist in Geneva. He declares the sacrament "was not ordained to be received only once a year . . . as now is the usual custom"[55] but should be received frequently. This means "the Supper could have been administered most becomingly if it were set before the church very often, and at least once a week."[56] Receiving communion this frequently was far too radical for the good burghers of Geneva, and Calvin lost. Earlier, he had tried for a monthly arrangement with each of the four parishes in Geneva celebrating at three-month intervals.[57] Calvin lost a major battle in failing to obtain frequent celebration of the eucharist.

The problem was the same everywhere; a weekly eucharist was familiar but weekly communion was far too radical, especially if preceding confession was expected. Cranmer's suppositions may have been a bit naive. In the 1549 rite, a rubric indicates that an encouragement to self-examination was to be read monthly "in Cathedral churches or other places where there is daily Communion. . . . And in parish churches, upon the week days it may be left unsaid." Such a rubric disappeared three years later. But the same exhortation is necessary as in 1549: if the people be "negligent to come to the holy Communion."[58] Obviously they were negligent, for 1552 bears a fateful rubric: "there shall be no celebration of the lord's Supper, except there be a good number to communicate with the Priest, according to his discretion." This is further refined as four or three at least. In cathedrals and collegiate churches, all clergy were to communicate "every Sunday at the least."[59]

Apparently what was happening was that not many communicants showed up weekly and an abbreviated service without the eucharist was mandated. Another rubric in 1552 prescribed that "every Parishioner shall communicate at the least three times in the year."[60] Fifty years later, the Canon Laws of 1604 recognized this occasional pattern by mandating that each parish celebrate the eucharist at least three times a year. As too often happens when a minimum is prescribed, that is what resulted. During the next two and a half centuries, Anglican bishops often pled in vain for one celebration in the long dry spell between Pentecost and Christmas. Anglicanism basically ceased to be a sacramental church for most of its history. In Anglican American churches the altar-table was a minor accessory, sometimes placed at the end where the slaves sat.

For many of the Puritans, this level of frequency was not enough. The First Church in Boston held the eucharist "once a month at the least." The *Westminster Directory* had stipulated that the "Supper of the Lord is frequently to be celebrated" but allowed each congregation to determine the frequency.[61] Some of the early Separatists (impatient reformers) had a weekly eucharist. For the Puritans it was requisite that there be a day set aside in the previous week for instruction and "due preparation," to prevent unworthy participation.

In the Kirk of Scotland, this led to the development by the late seventeenth century of "sacramental seasons." These were usually annual affairs involving several days of preparation for the celebration of the sacrament, a day for the eucharist, and a day of thanksgiving for what had been received. By going to adjoining parishes, one might receive the sacrament several times a year if one were willing to undergo the necessary discipline. Often this meant just one celebration per year per parish.[62] These sacramental seasons became one of the sources of the North American camp meeting beginning in 1800. Camp meetings in the early years climaxed with the eucharist for the new converts and the faithful and soon became annual affairs.

John Wesley preached a fervent sermon on "The Duty of Constant Communion." In what may not be a prime bit of exegesis, he says that when Jesus said "Do this" he meant do it as frequently as you can.[63] Wesley led by his example. Study of his journals shows that he received communion on the average of once every four or five days or seventy to ninety times a year.[64] He was frustrated by his fellow Anglican priests, who were content with the prevailing minimum of thrice yearly. In spreading the Methodist movement in America, Wesley's instructions were clear: "I also advise the elders to administer the supper of the Lord on every Lord's day."[65] Wesley's hopes were not fulfilled in America, partly due to the lack of ordained clergy. Traveling elders did preside at quarterly eucharists on their rounds of their circuits, often with large congregations.

Solutions to the problems of frequency and available clergy came on the frontier itself in the form of the Campbellite movement. Alexander Campbell, Barton Stone, and others became convinced that the biblical norm was a weekly eucharist. And they also determined that ordained clergy were not necessary. Out of this movement grew the Christian Churches (Disciples of Christ), the Churches of Christ, and others who came to practice a weekly eucharist on the basis of repristination, that is, recovering early Christianity. Influenced by a former Disciple, the Mormons also decided on a weekly eucharist. Thus on the American frontier in the 1830s, the long journey back to a frequent celebration of the eucharist began for Protestantism. At almost the same time, the Catholic revival in Church of England saw a return to more frequent celebrations. In Bavaria, Wilhelm Loehe began a long campaign to return to the norms of authentic Lutheran worship with confession before the eucharist and a weekly celebration.[66]

As the twentieth century began, Episcopalians were slowly moving to monthly celebrations. The Methodist Episcopal Church, South, mandated a monthly celebration by 1870, "wherever it is practicable." Methodists in the north were still accustomed to quarterly celebrations. And that was the situation in most Protestant churches. It was even formalized among Seventh-Day Adventists in speaking of Thirteenth Sabbaths as the proper time for quarterly communion.

Episcopal congregations gradually instituted an early morning eucharist on every Sunday. In England, the Parish Communion movement did much to make a single Sunday morning eucharist the norm.[67] As more and more Episcopal churches moved to a monthly eucharist, some Lutherans did likewise. Anglo-Catholic parishes quickly moved to a weekly eucharist, often non-communicating.

In the closing decades of the twentieth century, the process has accelerated. The 1970 Presbyterian *Worshipbook* assumed that the normal Service of the Lord's Day is the eucharist, anything else being deficient even though predominant. In many parts of the country, although not in much of the South, the Episcopal Church has now moved to a weekly eucharist as the norm. United Methodists, Presbyterians, and Lutherans are slowly moving in the same stream. There are a few United Methodist churches that have had a weekly eucharist as the only Sunday service for a quarter of a century or longer. They are the exception but more and more larger churches have the eucharist as one option on Sunday. The situation is similar with Presbyterians and Lutherans. Meanwhile, Disciples of Christ and Churches of Christ have kept every Lord's day with the Lord's Supper for nearly a century and three quarters.

PRESIDERS AT THE EUCHARIST

The question of the celebrant of the eucharist might seem simple, especially since most of the Reformers accepted the clerical culture of the medieval church. Ordained clergy, specifically priests, presbyters, or elders, were necessary to preside at the eucharist, and this assumption was rarely challenged.

Luther began with a functional concept of ministry. His most radical statement on the subject came in his 1520 treatise *To the Christian Nobility*. Hypothetically, a group of Christian laymen "set down in a desert without an episcopally ordained priest" could "elect one of their number, . . . charge him to baptize, say mass, . . . [and he] would be as truly a priest as though he had been ordained by all the bishops and popes in the world." He goes on to say that "there is no true, basic difference between laymen and priests."[68] But the actions of radicals soon led Luther to give thanks for the gift of ordained clergy, especially as preachers of God's Word. From 1525 on, he ordained pastors.[69]

Most of the other Reformers did likewise. Even the Anabaptists, who had a fairly quick turnover of clergy due to martyrdoms, usually considered an ordained man necessary for the eucharist. Groups as radical as the various English Separatists considered an ordained presider essential. When the New England Pilgrims' pastor, John Robinson, a priest of the Church of England, failed to migrate with them to Plymouth, they went without the eucharist for nine years until another priest could join them. Only the Quakers, by eliminating both clergy and the eucharist, settled the problem.

John Wesley was plagued by the unavailability of ordained Anglican priests to celebrate the eucharist for the people called Methodists. Sometimes the people even crowded into sickrooms in order to share communion with the sick. When past eighty years of age, Wesley yielded to necessity and ordained elders and a superintendent for his followers in America. He had become convinced that a continuous apostolic succession through bishops alone was a pious fiction, a view which modern scholarship seems to uphold. But his ordinal for America included three rites: deacon, elder, and "superintendant." Wesley was distressed when two of the leaders of the church in America assumed the title of bishop. Wesley's concern for America was clear: "For some hundred miles together there is none either to baptize or to administer the Lord's Supper."[70] His solution, the right-wing answer, was to be flexible and ordain more presbyters (elders).

An alternate response to the problem of celebrating the eucharist regularly on the American frontier where there were no clergy for many miles developed half a century later. The 1830s were a time of Jacksonian democracy, and liturgical democracy finally arrived on the American frontier among the followers of Alexander Campbell and Barton Stone. If, as they argued, the Lord's Supper "is an instituted part of the worship and edification of all Christian congregations in all their stated meetings,"[71] then who was to preside on the frontier? The answer was clear: senior laymen could preside. Here was the left-wing approach: go beyond clergy. Mormons adopted a somewhat different approach, making most laymen priests of one sort or another. And the Plymouth Brethren encouraged lay presiders at their weekly eucharists. Base communities in many parts of the world today have followed this approach despite rules in Catholicism and much of Protestantism against lay presiders.

In 1853, a small Congregational church in South Butler, New York, ordained Antoinette Brown (later Blackwell) as pastor to preach and preside over their eucharist. This was only five years after the Seneca Falls Woman's Rights Convention and only a few miles away. Given a theological education, but not a degree, at Oberlin College, she was the first ordained woman in a major denomination to preside at the eucharist. But since then, especially after 1956, when women clergy received full rights in The Methodist Church, women have become presiders at the eucharist in many churches.

For most churches, presiding at the eucharist still remains a clerical prerogative. Perhaps the witness of the younger churches of the world will change this in the twenty-first century, perhaps not. Except for good order, ordination does not seem to bear any intrinsic relation to the eucharist.

THE PARTICIPATION OF COMMUNICANTS

In late medieval Christianity in the West, the congregation was a dispensable item. Thousands of masses were said each day for the repose of the dead in what were essentially private masses. Luther obviously found this deplorable, but it was not until 1533 that he devoted an entire treatise to decrying the private mass. Private masses, he said, are contrary to "Christ's ordinance and intention . . . [for] one should administer the sacrament and preach about him [Christ] in order to strengthen the faith." Instead the priests use the masses to "sell for money."[72]

For Luther, not only must a congregation be present but it must hear the word and receive communion under both elements. Debate had gone on in the previous century about the laity receiving the chalice and some temporary concessions had been precedents in allowing the laity to receive in both species in parts of Bohemia. Three elements stand out in Luther's reform of the mass: a congregation must be present, it must hear the preaching of the Word, and it must be able to participate in the eucharist. The private mass was quickly abolished in Lutheran circles. Luther began energetic reforms to increase both the quantity and quality of preaching of the Word, especially through publishing collections of sermons, the postils.

Participation came about through several reforms. In 1523 Luther published his *Formula Missae*, the mass as reformed in Wittenberg. Rather amazingly, it is still in Latin. Others had anticipated the vernacular by as much as two years, beginning with Andreas Carlstadt's Christmas mass in Wittenberg in 1521. Luther celebrated in German in 1525 and published his German Mass in 1526.[73] Basically it is a conservative revision of the Latin mass except for the canon, which is reduced to Christ's words of institution. The elements are consecrated and administered separately and the elevation is retained. All are to receive both the bread and the wine, the women after the men. Ceremonial is to be simplified and many elements of "tomfoolery" eliminated.

A major advance was Luther's efforts to introduce congregational hymnody, beginning with the publication of a small hymnal in 1524 containing German hymns already in use in Wittenberg. Each year the number of hymns increased, Luther himself often serving as both writer and composer. Thirty-seven hymns[74] attributed to him have survived, including "A Mighty Fortress," written and composed about 1528. He encouraged others to write and compose with such success that even today Lutherans are distinguished by the abundance of music in their services.

The result is that Lutheran worship and all subsequent Protestant worship took on a highly oral character. Participation was seen largely as a matter of the mouth and ears, although seeing was not neglected.[75] One is always astonished in visiting Lutheran countries after traveling in England and Scotland to find how much there is of visual interest in Lutheran buildings. But preaching is also a highly visual act. Many efforts were made, beginning with Luther, to place the altar-table so that the communicants could see the actions of the priest as well as hear his words. From 1526 on, virtually everything was celebrated in the vernacular wherever the Reformation prevailed, except in Sweden. Indeed, the liturgies and other writings of Luther, Calvin, and Cranmer did much to shape the modern development of German, French, and English.

When it came to communion, there was a major exception: it did not include infants and children. The Council of Trent acknowledged that children had been communed in earlier ages for reasons that seemed sufficient then.[76] But Catholics and Protestants alike took steps to dissuade children from communion. For Anabaptists it was not an issue, for children could not be baptized and so could not commune until old enough to be considered believers.

In the Church of England, communion of children was effectively prevented by requiring knowledge of the catechism and then confirmation before first communion. The final rubric in the 1549 confirmation rite says, "And there shall none be admitted to the holy communion until such time as he be confirmed." The 1552 rite adds the further condition "as he can say the Catechism."[77]

Though the Puritans did not care for confirmation, they still found it necessary to insist on a public profession of faith before children were admitted to communion. There was also a further limitation: "The Ignorant and the Scandalous are not fit to receive this Sacrament of the Lords Supper."[78] Ultimately, the Puritans are reflecting Calvin's prohibition against the unworthy communicant and Paul's stern warning to the Corinthians (1 Cor. 11:27) that whoever partakes unworthily "will be answerable for the body and blood of the Lord." Calvin had sought to prevent unworthy communicants by the practice of the "fencing of tables." He fulminates against unworthy partakers, who receive poison instead of nourishment and "are estranged from and out of accord with their brethren."[79] Perfection is not requisite, but faith and love are. According to Calvin's practice, elders visited in homes to make certain that faith prevailed. At various times, the Reformed and Methodist traditions have used communion tokens or tickets as evidence for admissibility to the sacrament. In Puritan New England, public profession of faith and owning the local church covenant were necessary for receiving communion.

Various forms of closed communion have survived, ranging from limiting communion only to members of a particular denomination to restricting it only to members of a local congregation. On the other hand, proponents of "open" communion usually welcome all baptized Christians. A proposal among Presbyterians in the 1970s even suggested welcoming the unbaptized who were present, but this was defeated.

A new dimension has appeared in recent years in debates over the communion of children. The 1980s and 1990s have seen a new concern about baptism in many churches, expressed through the formation of various study commissions and publications. Out of this has come a concern in the pedobaptist churches for the communion of baptized children as a logical consequence of their initiation into the Christian community. The debate has many ingredients. Early on, Urban Holmes, in *Young Children and the Eucharist*,[80] used developmental psychology as a basis for arguing that although children think relationally, that is not sufficient to bar them from the table until they think cognitively.

Others have used a historical argument. In the West, until the twelfth century, children were regularly communed with wine at their baptism; the East has communicated children throughout history.[81] Others found more persuasive a theological argument: baptism places one within the church fully and completely, so exclusion from the Lord's table simply because of age is an illicit form of excommunication.[82] This has further implications in terms of those with mental disabilities. Is the ability to think rationally a prerequisite for receiving communion?[83] With the downplaying of confirmation in many churches, it seems most likely that communion of children will increasingly become common in churches that baptize children.

THE COMMUNION ELEMENTS

The eucharist involves physical elements and actions. Therefore we must look briefly at the actual bread and wine that become the basis of Christ's presence in this sacrament.

For most of history, both the bread and wine have been given to communicants and they still are in the East. But in the West, growing scrupulosity about the possibility of spilling the wine led, from the twelfth century onwards, to restricting the wine to the priest. The doctrine of concomitance was developed to claim that the whole Christ was received in a single fragment of bread regardless of size. In the fifteenth century, Jan Hus had urged that the cup be given to the laity and concessions to this effect were made for a limited time in Bohemia by the Council of Basel in 1533.

For Luther, withholding the cup from the laity is the first captivity of the eucharist. Christ has clearly ordained, "Drink from it, all of you" (Matt. 26:27) and the church has no right to alter what Christ has commanded. "It is wicked and despotic," he claims, "to deny both kinds to the laity, and . . . this is not within the power of any angel, much less of any pope or council."[84] Communion under both kinds rapidly became universal in Protestantism and has become general practice among Roman Catholics in recent years despite Trent's declaration that this was not obligatory "by any divine precept."[85]

The ordinary form of the bread in the West had been unleavened bread; in the East, leavened bread was and still is used. Apparently the Western pattern survived among some Protestants. Zwingli's rite of 1525 specifies unleavened bread. But he also mandated that "the plates and cups are of wood, that pomp may not come back again."[86] People were now eating and drinking from the same vessels they were familiar with at home. This must have made a profound statement in a non-verbal fashion. And they received it in the pews by breaking off a piece of bread and drinking from the cup.

The same use of unleavened bread is indicated by Cranmer in 1549: "that is to say, unleavened, and round, as it was afore, but without all manner of print, and something more larger and thicker than it was, so that it may be aptly divided in divers pieces." The minister was to break it into at least two pieces and thus distribute it and it is affirmed that the "whole Body" of Christ is in each piece. A strange concern about finances intrudes as it is enacted that the parish must pay for the cost of the "holy loaf." But a major change came about in three years. The 1552 book decrees that in order to "take away the superstition, which any person hath, . . . it shall suffice that the bread be such, as is usual to be eaten at the Table with other meats, but the best and purest wheat bread, that conveniently may be gotten." Presumably this means ordinary leavened bread "of finest wheat." Furthermore, "If any of the bread or wine remain, the Curate shall have it to his own use." In other words, after the eucharist, the loaf is treated as once again ordinary bread.[87]

The laity, of course, are to receive from the chalice, too. Obviously, much more wine was necessary than when the priest alone drank. Woodcuts of Anglican altar-tables from the eighteenth century frequently show two or more large flagons used to refill the chalices used. In 1549, the rubric says, "giving every one to drink once and no more" as if necessary to prevent over-indulgence. Such precaution disappeared in 1552.[88]

The 1549 prayer book permitted taking consecrated bread and wine to the sick room on the day of the parish eucharist. Even this very limited form of reserved sacrament disappeared in 1552, as it was decreed that the consecration must take place in the sickroom so that all present might hear the words of the gospel. Not until the Catholic revival of the nineteenth century did a reserved sacrament in the church again become possible among Anglicans.

Cranmer retained in 1549 mixing into the wine "a little pure and clean water,"[89] but this provision lapsed in 1552. The mixture of water and wine was probably originally necessary to make first-century wine drinkable. By the third century, it had come to symbolize the mixture of Christ and us (Cyprian) as well as the flow from Christ's wound. John Wesley revived the practice in the eighteenth century and the Tractarians in the nineteenth.

For the Mormons in Utah in 1847, water was abundant but wine was not. So they began, and continue, to use water instead of wine, a practice known in a fourth-century sect, the Aquarians.

In 1869, a pious Methodist dentist, Thomas Welch, invented a means of pasteurizing grape juice so as to prevent fermentation. This coincided with the first great feminist crusade, that of temperance, which meant total abstention from alcohol. Beginning in 1876, Methodists Disciplines recommended and then mandated the use of "pure unfermented juice of the grape" at the eucharist. Such a prohibition lasted until 1988. Many other American churches also switched to grape juice and many continue to use it today. In the thirteenth century, Bishop Durandus had accepted the use of fresh pressed (i.e., unfermented) grape juice as valid. Alcoholic Catholic priests can receive permission to use it today. Perhaps these points can be resolved with the advent of nonalcoholic wines.

Whatever else they believe, Americans believe devoutly in germs. In 1894, members of Central Presbyterian Church in Rochester, New York, became convinced that only by using small individual communion glasses could people come to the eucharist without fear.[90] So individual glasses became common. This provoked a reaction in some Church of Christ congregations as unbiblical, and a brief "one chalice" movement ensued. An alternative to the glasses is the practice of intinction, which has become common in many churches.

In the black churches, baking the communion bread is considered a distinct ministry. Recipes are often passed down from generation to generation and give certain families an important role in the congregation.

Modern liturgical reform has made the breaking of the bread an important act in the eucharist ever since Gregory Dix identified the fraction as one of the four great actions of the liturgy.[91] This has led to widespread adoption of leavened bread that may be broken and tastes and looks like real bread. The convenience of the little wafers is not matched by the sign value of real bread as Christ's coming to us in the midst of the ordinary. Thus increasingly there is a move to the use of real bread and real wine in terms that relate to modern cultures wherever one is in the world. This poses daunting problems in cultures where bread or grape wine are unknown. As yet these problems have not been satisfactorily resolved.

CHAPTER FIVE

Eucharistic Meanings

Over the centuries, the eucharist has borne a wide variety of mean-ings at different times and places. The center of gravity among these has shifted several times. The most obvious conclusion is that a single definition is insufficient; the eucharist has many meanings. Our purpose is to discover those meanings that have had the strongest appeal to various Protestants during nearly five centuries of practices and controversies.

We shall organize this inquiry on the basis of categories expressed in 1926 by the Swedish Lutheran Archbishop of Uppsala, Yngve Brilioth. His book *Eucharistic Faith and Practice, Evangelical and Catholic*[1] is one of the classics of twentieth-century liturgical studies along with others by Joseph Jungmann[2] and Gregory Dix.[3] Obvious-ly, much has changed in seventy or more years and we cannot be quite content with the list of four metaphors plus real presence (which we have already treated) that he left. From our vantage point, he over-looked the eschatological context and neglected the eucharist as the work of the Holy Spirit. Nor shall we interpret the four metaphors exactly as might have been done in the 1920s. But it is interesting that these metaphors are largely duplicated by the meanings that *Baptism, Eucharist and Ministry* more recently (1982) extracted from the eucharist. Sacrifice was omitted as still too hot an issue for ecumenical agreement.

The five metaphors we shall examine are the eucharist as thanksgiving, commemoration, communion, sacrifice, and the work of the Holy Spirit. There five metaphors all interlock. They are not opposites or opponents but all complement each other. However, relative emphases have shifted and we shall try to chronicle these changes.

THE ESCHATOLOGICAL CONTEXT

The context of the eucharist in the New Testament is highly eschatological. Even the words at the Last Supper indicate a strong sense of the imminent coming of the kingdom. The words of institution include "until it is fulfilled in the kingdom of God" or "until the kingdom of God comes" (Luke 22:16, 18). Even the kingdom is seen in terms of table fellowship: "so that you may eat and drink at my table in my kingdom" (Luke 22:30). Paul makes the Lord's Supper even more an anticipation: "For as often as you eat this bread and drink the cup, you proclaim the Lord's death until he comes" (1 Cor. 11:26).

There is a strong sense of the imminent return of the Lord and the beginning of the kingdom of which the Lord's Supper is a foretaste, an anticipation. The Supper sums up all God's work in creation and redemption and moves on to final consummation. And it helps the Christian to participate in this final stage of salvation, albeit in a limited way. At the same time, each celebration invokes and advances the coming of the kingdom both by prayer and by anticipation.[4]

Yet this faith, so fervent in the early church's experience of the eucharist, faded away with the passing of time. The imminent coming of the kingdom ceased to be an important part of piety except for occasional radical movements. Eschatology was not part of the inheritance of the Reformers, and few of them missed it. For over a thousand years, it had been neglected. It is not strange that eschatology appears rarely in the Reformation.

The chief exception is some Anabaptists who lived in millennial expectation. Persecution only served to heighten the sense of living in the last days. In the eucharist, the "inner communion" of a pure church pointed beyond itself to the final culmination. The eucharist was an anticipation of feasting in the Kingdom.

The magisterial reformation was more inclined to look to the present than into the future. Not until we get to Wesley in the eighteenth century do eschatological references multiply. No less than twenty-three of the eucharistic hymns are in a section entitled "The Sacrament a Pledge of Heaven." The first of these rhapsodizes:

> Even now the marriage-feast we share,
>   Even now we by the Lamb are fed;
>   Our Lord's celestial joy we prove.[5]

These words come after a verse reminiscent of the *Dies irae*, "the dreadful joyful day." The image of the wedding feast is frequent in this section, as well as "Maranatha": "Come quickly, Lord, . . . prepare the bride, and then return." The saints above join in the never ending feast and we aspire "till to the holiest place we rise / And keep the feast for ever there."[6]

Various nineteenth-century movements picked up these themes. The Catholic Apostolic Church was a deeply apocalyptic movement in England and beyond. The conclusion of its eucharistic prayer begins, "Hasten, O God, the time when Thou shall send from Thy right hand," and ends invoking the day when we "shall be presented with exceeding joy before the presence of the glory."[7] Apocalyptic themes also appeared among the Adventist churches and the Mormons. Modern-day Pentecostals often sound deeply eschatological with their worship heavily imbued with the present activity of the Holy Spirit. These gifts of the spirit indicate the imminent return of Christ.

In recent decades, mainline churches have picked up eschatological themes. Part of this is the result of historical and biblical scholarship. Gregory Dix's *Shape of the Liturgy* documents the strong eschatology of the early eucharist. Dix claimed that in the fourth century the church "became reconciled to *time*. The eschatological emphasis in the eucharist inevitably faded."[8] It was replaced by a backward historical direction. Probably this had already happened long before, but Dix and others pointed out the losses involved.

Baptism, Eucharist and Ministry approaches eschatology through the image of "The Eucharist as Meal of the Kingdom" and points out that it culminates in mission to the entire world. A feature of most modern eucharistic rites is the acclamation: "Christ has died; Christ is risen; Christ will come again." The United Methodist eucharistic prayer anticipates "until Christ comes in final victory / and we feast at his heavenly banquet."[9] Various Episcopal prayers read, "Bring us with all your saints / into the joy of your eternal kingdom" or "as we await the day of his coming."[10] This theme is less apparent in the Lutheran rite. The Presbyterians embellish "as we await the day of his coming" with the alternative "until Christ comes in final victory / and we shall feast with all your saints / in the joy of your eternal realm."[11] A nice touch picks up on the *Didache's* first-century reference to the bread "scattered upon the hills" (9:4) by praying "so may your church be gathered / from the ends of the earth into your kingdom." A concluding prayer thanks God for having "given us a foretaste of the heavenly banquet / in your eternal kingdom."[12] "Great Thanksgiving E" is even more emphatic in its vision of when "his coming in glory [may] find us."[13]

THE EUCHARIST AS THANKSGIVING

The English word *eucharist* derives from the Greek verb *eucharistéo*, "give thanks, render or return thanks." It is closely related to the giving of praise. In the New Testament, Jesus gives thanks at the Last Supper. Very early on, to give thanks meant to celebrate the Lord's Supper, as in the *Didache* (9 and 14). The "breaking of bread" (Acts 2:46) and the "Supper of the Lord" are similar expressions.

For first-century Jews, *giving thanks* and *blessing* are closely related terms. And much of it is done in the context of reciting those historical acts of God for which one gives thanks. Thus one blesses God for creation, deliverance, and a whole series of beneficial events. To give thanks is a joyful activity in which one rejoices, usually with others who share the same common happy memories. Acts 2:46-7 speaks of the Jerusalem church as breaking bread together "with glad and generous hearts, praising God." An implication of thanksgiving, then, is rejoicing together for common benefits.

This aspect had certainly become muted in the medieval low mass. Aside from the *Gloria in excelsis*, preface, and *Sanctus*, all in Latin, thanksgiving was a relatively minor theme for medieval piety. What had sprouted in the medieval period was a number of apologies for the sinfulness of the presider and community. The pervading spirit was one of penitential gloom, focusing on the unworthiness of those present rather than the supreme worth of God. The mass had become a highly individualistic groveling before God because of human sin. It is no accident that the chief image in many late medieval churches was the painting of the last judgment over the chancel arch. There is little joy there for the damned.

It is not surprising that the metaphor of thanksgiving does not reappear immediately in the Reformation, although Melanchthon can speak of prayer as the "sacrifice of thanksgiving" or the Word as "sacrifices of praise" in the *Apology of the Augsburg Confession*.[14] Luther's truncation of the canon of the mass eliminates one opportunity for developing this aspect, except that he includes a German *Sanctus*. For Luther, thanksgiving seems largely focused on the element of the promise of forgiveness of sin. Christ's body and blood are given "*for you* for the forgiveness of sins" because "in the sacrament you receive from Christ's lips the forgiveness of sins."[15]

This atmosphere is changed by Luther's hymns such as "Dear Christians, Let us now rejoice, / And dance in joyous measure" (1523) or "Let God be blest, be praised, and be thanked, / Who to us himself hath granted" (1524).[16] The introduction of hymns sung by the congregation signifies new outbursts of giving thanks on the part of the people.

This possibility Zwingli did not favor as he eliminated congregational singing altogether although he did propose antiphonal reading of Psalm 113, "Praise, O servants of the Lord," in addition to the *Gloria in excelsis*. The Anabaptists did not have the same inhibitions about congregational song, and hymnody became a major ingredient of their celebrations of the eucharist. Many of the hymns were heavily penitential, but they must have added a thankful note of joy to the occasion.

Calvin's service is so morally earnest that there is not much room for thanksgiving. Even the concluding "Thanksgiving After the Supper" puts in a plea for good behavior. Calvin did introduce congregational singing of the psalms, and visitors to Geneva found this radiant and joyful. But one gets a different view from his theology than from his rite. In a brilliant book, Brian Gerrish has shown how central to Calvin's theology is "gratitude for God's gifts."[17] The Lord's Supper is a gift in which we receive Christ himself through the Holy Spirit. Though nervous about the concept of sacrifice, Calvin finds abundant scriptural proof that in "the Lord's supper . . . we proclaim his death and give thanks, we do nothing but offer a sacrifice of praise."[18] Calvin speaks of the need to celebrate the Lord's Supper "with fitting praises and to celebrate it with thanksgiving"[19] and at its end, "thanks should be given, and praises sung to God."[20] Calvin opposes any sense that "this sacrifice is truly propitiatory," as reiterated by the Council of Trent.[21] But Calvin seizes on passages, such as Hebrews 13:15, that speak of a "sacrifice of praise."

Cranmer certainly approves of the sacrifice of praise, but judging from modern standards his eucharist is a pretty sober affair. His 1549 rite begins with the *Gloria in excelsis*, but in 1552 this has been moved to a spot after all have communed. In this location, thanksgiving for what has been received is perhaps even stronger. Cranmer retains five proper prefaces which highlight the work of the Trinity on the five occasions of commemoration. And, of course, the *Sanctus* is a hymn of praise. The "Sacrifice of praise and thanksgiving" is mentioned in the oblation which became a postcommunion prayer in 1552. The 1549 post-communion prayer is definitely one of thanksgiving and becomes an alternative prayer in 1552. Either leads to the *Gloria in excelsis*. Cranmer lamented the lack of poets to write English hymns, but in 1552 he also eliminated the introits, largely from psalms, which had prefaced the eucharist in 1549.

The Puritans, when in power, instructed that "the Prayer, Thanksgiving, or Blessing of the Bread and Wine" should "give thanks to God for all his benefits, . . . and for this Sacrament in particular, by which Christ and all his benefits are applied and sealed up unto us, . . . after so much and long abuse of them all."[22] We can only hope that the Almighty was not subjected to too much theological polemic in these prayers.

There is a very strong view of thanksgiving in many of the Wesleys' eucharistic hymns. Rattenbury speaks of many of the hymns as "A Protestant Crucifix" in their insistence on portraying Christ as dying for our salvation. One of the best marvels, "O the depth of love Divine, / Th' unfathomable grace!"[23] Many, especially those in the section "After the Sacrament," rejoice in the joys of the blessed united to Christ in this way.

The recovery of the splendor of ceremonial and architecture in the Catholic Revival in the Church of England is a nonverbal form of expressing gratitude. Proponents of the Oxford Movement often argued that recovered ceremonial gave the poor an opportunity to experience joy and beauty so often lacking in their drab lives.

102

Much the same instinct was expressed in American revivalism in the multitude of hymns to express one's closeness to Jesus. In the earlier phases, much of this was linked to the eucharist and the experience of the king come into the camp. This was less the case by the twentieth century, when "blessed assurance" had few eucharistic overtones.

For the Pentecostals, there often were ecstatic praises of God at the celebration of the eucharist, but the presence of Christ was a vivid experience whether the eucharist was celebrated or not.

Recent decades have seen some major shifts in a move to stressing the joyful aspects of the eucharist as thanksgiving in the reformed rites of Protestants and Catholics alike. Biblical studies have changed our attitude to Judaism and made us realize the strong continuity of Jewish worship and early Christian worship. In particular, the Jewish means of giving thanks by reciting God's saving acts has come to the forefront. Studies of ancient Christian liturgies have helped to emphasize this indebtedness to Judaism.

Theological shifts have contributed much, too. Most of the people charged with liturgical revision in the major Protestant churches came out of a neoorthodox theology heavily tempered by the biblical theology of the 1950s and 1960s. In their theological journeys, many were touched by liberation theology. For many, the belief that the paschal mystery of the death and resurrection of Christ is the center of Christianity had given a new focus to Christian faith. They were seeking an objectivity that the pre–World War II liberalism, with its heavily subjective emphasis, could not supply. Thanksgiving has an objective character because its focus is beyond the human and addresses the divine.

Thus it is not surprising that *Baptism, Eucharist and Ministry* places "The Eucharist as Thanksgiving to the Father" as the first topic under the meaning of the eucharist. That must have been an easy consensus.

If we look at the new eucharistic rites, the central prayer is no longer called "The Prayer of Consecration" as in the 1662 *Book of Common Prayer*, it is rather "The great thanksgiving." And the contents certainly substantiate this new nomenclature. They relish the recital of God's saving acts. In The United Methodist Church, there are now twenty-four eucharistic prayers officially approved, all stressing thanksgiving.[24] The Episcopal Church weighs in with six great thanksgivings.[25] Lutherans now have five great thanksgivings plus the words of institution.[26] Presbyterians have twenty-five great thanksgivings plus an outline, all with a heavy emphasis on praise and thanksgiving.[27] Certainly the tide has turned in the direction of emphasizing the eucharist as thanksgiving. What seems newest is actually, as so often happens, also the oldest layer in the Christian tradition.

THE EUCHARIST AS COMMEMORATION

There is a very close relationship between thanksgiving and commemoration. This may not have been so apparent in Brilioth's time (he discusses communion next after thanksgiving) but is one of the most important liturgical discoveries of the last half-century. Once again this has come about through acknowledgment of the Jewish roots of Christian worship. Gregory Dix is reputed to have said in a speech in Grapevine, Texas, in the late 1940s that the most important liturgical discovery in recent years was that Jesus was a Jew. This was obvious, but the liturgical implications were less so.

Jewish thanksgiving involved a recital of God's saving acts. Thus we thank God by reiterating what God has done for God's people. Salvation history is narrated in order to give thanks. Beginning with creation, moving on to the present, and involving supplication for the future, Jewish prayer covers the whole sweep of history. It is grateful praise of all God's works and invocation for those yet to come, such as restoring the glory of Jerusalem. In the process of commemorating these events, their power to save again becomes present. The passover is reenacted as if we were contemporaries of the escape from slavery, and yet it also looks to future culmination.

Christians have come to realize that when Luke and Paul use the term *anámnesis* in the words of Jesus at the Last Supper, they are speaking of something much stronger than "in remembrance of me," something which defies our ability to translate in its full meaning. *Anámnesis* suggests the power to experience anew the reality of Christ. Commemoration thus has the power of reliving the event in all its power to save and it frees us from our captivity to the present by making all God's saving acts present for us to appropriate.

The eucharistic prayers of the early church tend to depict the sweep of salvation history beginning with the creation. The most comprehensive of these appears in book 8 of the *Apostolic Constitutions*, compiled about 375, which narrates salvation history from creation to second coming, even including the ten plagues of Egypt.[28] In the East, eucharistic prayers still begin with the creation and narrate God's subsequent acts. But the West long ago lost interest in narrating the events of the Old Covenant. Its interest in the eucharist became increasingly focused on the events beginning with the day before Christ suffered. Because the words of institution were considered the moment of consecration, commemoration focused heavily on the passion, death, and resurrection. Visually, Christ on the cross became a dominant focus of the church, whether above the roodscreen or at the altar-table. Commemoration in the West had been largely narrowed to the passion, death, and resurrection. The Old Testament reading had long disappeared and creation was hardly mentioned save in the creed.

It is not surprising then, that the Reformers' approach to commemoration was as narrow as what they inherited. If anything, Luther's elimination of most of the eucharistic prayer save the words of institution had the effect of narrowing the commemoration even further. However, the German *Sanctus*, which follows, does recall the Isaiah 6 passage. Fortunately, the vernacular hymns, many based on the psalms, expand the scope of commemoration a bit. The traditional epistle and gospel were retained, but the Old Testament lesson was not recovered. The medieval passion focus still prevailed.

Zwingli's 1523 *Attack on the Canon of the Mass* does narrate the creation and the fall.[29] But this is lost in his eucharistic rite of 1525. The Anabaptist imagination did not seem to go further either.

One recovery, unfortunate from our point of view, from the Old Testament was Martin Bucer's effort in Strasbourg to append the Ten Commandments to the beginning of the eucharist as an act of self-examination. This induced Calvin to have them sung by the congregation and Cranmer to add them to the 1552 eucharist, whence they passed into the Methodist tradition until 1965. From Elizabeth I to Victoria, the most conspicuous item in Anglican churches was the decalogue, creed, and Lord's Prayer painted on tablets above the altar-table.

The focus of Cranmer's eucharistic rites is heavily on Calvary. There is slight reference even to the resurrection, although the five proper prefaces do expand the vision slightly on their occasions and the week following (Christmas, Easter, Ascension, Whitsunday, and Trinity). As morning and evening prayer gradually became the norm for Sunday and daily worship, the Old Testament reappeared daily in two lessons, the psalms, and the canticles. Perhaps this reinforced the

Puritan interest in the reading of the totality of Scripture. The New England Puritans saw themselves in Old Testament terms and the new world as a New Canaan or a New Ark. Hence they could think of the eucharist in covenant terms and restrict it to those within the ecclesiastical covenant.

The first segment of the Wesleys' eucharistic hymns (27 in all) is entitled "As it is a Memorial of the Sufferings and Death of Christ." Part 3 is "The Sacrament a Pledge of Heaven." Even though Old Testament imagery is present, especially in part 4 on sacrifice, the medieval passion piety still prevails. And that seems to have been the focus in most Protestant eucharistic piety at least until the late twentieth century. The eucharist seemed to focus almost entirely on the passion, death, and resurrection, with the second coming occasionally mentioned.

A major revolution in the way we see the eucharist as commemoration has occurred among both Protestants and Catholics in recent decades. The concept of commemoration has been expanded to include all of salvation history past, present, and pressing on to the second coming. There have been many factors leading to this new approach.

Biblical studies have tended to stress the continuity of the Old and New Testaments. Many themes pervade both testaments. Historical studies have reminded us how seriously many early eucharistic liturgies took the old covenant, pairing creation with redemption. In theological terms, the work of Odo Casel, O.S.B., has had a profound significance.[30] Casel believed that what happens in the liturgy is that the community relives sacred history for itself. Thus the Christian year and daily office become cycles of re-experiencing the whole of salvation history. Casel got his approach from a study of ancient mystery religions; we now see this as endemic in the Hebrew Bible itself. And the steadfast witness of the eastern churches to the whole sequence of salvation history has not been overlooked.

Another factor in our consciousness is the environmental movement beginning in the 1970s. Few pictures have had as profound an impact on human consciousness as that of the whole earth taken from space in 1969. Creation, we now realize, is coordinate with redemption. So there has been a paradigm shift in much Christian thinking about God's work on our behalf.

This shift has had a profound impact on how we approach the

whole metaphor of the eucharist as commemoration. *Baptism, Eucharist and Ministry* interprets the eucharist "as the great thanksgiving to the Father for everything accomplished in creation, redemption and sanctification . . . and . . . in bringing the Kingdom to fulfillment."[31] The theme of *anámnesis* as both representation and anticipation is strong. The dimensions of history commemorated have broadened exponentially from that salvation to which Western Christians have been accustomed.

This becomes very obvious when one looks at the new eucharistic rites as well as many recent eucharistic hymns. The preface of the United Methodist rite gives thanks and praise for creation and for God's steadfast love in the face of the fall, in deliverance from captivity, in making covenant, and in sending the prophets.[32] The Episcopal rite provides twenty-two proper prefaces for various occasions. Most impressive is Eucharistic Prayer C, sometimes known as the "Star Wars" prayer. It exults in "interstellar space, galaxies, suns, the planets in their courses, and this fragile earth." And then it details our creation, fall, prophets, sages, and the law.[33] Prayer D, which is based on St. Basil's rite of Alexandria, refers to creation, fall, and covenant.[34]

The Lutheran rite mentions creation, Abraham, and the prophets in the first eucharist prayer.[35] Coming last in composition, the Presbyterian great thanksgivings relish images of creation, rebellion, and prophets.[36] All of these new prayers rush on from commemoration of the past to hope for the completion of all things in the coming of Christ in final victory. The scope of commemoration has drastically increased in all the new rites.

THE EUCHARIST AS COMMUNION

The eucharist is described in the New Testament as *koinonía*, that is, as communion or fellowship. Paul speaks of "a sharing *[koinonía]* in the blood of Christ" and "a sharing *[koinonía]* in the body of Christ" and continues, "Because there is one bread, we who are many are one body, for we all partake of the one bread" (1 Cor. 10:16-17). Baptism places us in the one body, and it is necessary to discern the Lord's body in unity. All this relates to the Jewish sense of the unity of those eating together. A sign of this unity became the kiss of peace (2 Cor. 13:12).

Unfortunately, over the centuries this strong corporate sense tended to dissipate, especially in the West. There were a number of factors contributing to this, not the least of which was the infrequency of the receiving of communion by the laity. From the Fourth Lateran Council (1215) through the Council of Trent (1545–1563) it was necessary to legislate that people should receive at least once a year at Easter. Partaking "of the one bread" was infrequent. The kiss of peace became completely clericalized.

A chief contributing factor was that the mass was in a language no one understood (often including the priest). It was no longer a communal activity. People attended mass basically to say their own private devotions in the company of others and to glimpse the host at the elevation. There was no common liturgical activity. Devotions were done in the context of a completely clericalized liturgy. People did not sing or pray together. In short, devotions had replaced liturgy for the people.

It is very likely that the chief positive gain of the Reformation in worship was the possibility of restoring the liturgy in place of devotions. Even such a title as *The Book of Common Prayer* must have sounded oxymoronic because common folk did not have books, nor did they pray together. The essence of the Roman Catholic reforms since Vatican II has been to replace devotions during the liturgy (such as the rosary) with the involvement by the people in "full conscious and active participation." Praying, singing, and hearing the Word of God together, as well as communing, was the essence of liturgy for the Reformers.

Most of the Reformers' liturgical ideals were tied directly to the rest of their theology. In Luther's case, the priesthood of all believers was basic. But even he was behind others in catching the full implications of everyone being able to share in the liturgy by singing and praying in a common language. Others had anticipated Luther on the issue of the vernacular by a few years or months.[37] His *Formula Missae* of 1523 was still in Latin but on October 29, 1525, Luther celebrated in German, and he published his German Mass in January 1526. From that point on, almost all Protestant liturgies were in German, French, English, and other languages.

Luther's efforts to abolish the private mass were based on the need for a common participation; private liturgy became unthinkable. The development of vernacular hymnody and service music was another means to make liturgy truly public. Luther moved from liturgical music sung by professionals to musical liturgy sung by the people together. And every mass was to be accompanied by preaching so that everyone could hear the Word of God interpreted. Everyone was expected to commune regularly and to receive both bread and wine. Non-communicating masses were abolished.

Much that Luther set in motion became irrevocable in Protestantism. The eucharist was to focus on the communion of the whole assembly. For Zwingli, the sense of fellowship was central. The whole purpose of the eucharist was for the assembly to experience Christ's spiritual presence by remembering him together. Whereas Luther focused on transformed bread and wine, Zwingli looked at transformed worshipers. The ecclesial dimension for Zwingli was central; Christ was experienced in the gathered community. Christ was present and active in the community but not in the bread and wine. As Zwingli says:

> When we poor creatures observe this act of thanksgiving amongst ourselves, we all confess that we are of those who believe in the Lord Jesus Christ, and seeing this confession is demanded of us all, all who keep the remembrance or thanksgiving are one body with all other Christians. Therefore if we are the members of his body, it is most necessary that we should live together as Christians.[38]

The sacrament as means of professing faith was key to Zwingli; both baptism and the eucharist are public acts proclaiming the community's faith.

This reached its highest intensity among the Anabaptists. They celebrated the eucharist of a pure community in which all present were risking their lives even to be there. They broke bread together, never knowing who might be martyred next for such an act of defying civil authority. Conrad Grebel, a lay leader of the Swiss Brethren (Anabaptists) pointed out that the elements are "to show us that we are truly one bread and one body, and that we are and wish to be true brethren with one another. . . . The Supper is an expression of fellowship, not a Mass and sacrament. Therefore none is to receive it alone, neither on his deathbed nor otherwise."[39] Those "who will not live the brotherly life" should not be allowed to partake; they lack the inner bond of love, so the outer bond of bread is meaningless. According to the

Schleitheim Confession of 1527, all those who commune "must beforehand be united in the one body of Christ." Only those truly united in Christ may "be made one loaf together."[40]

So intense was this sense of fellowship among the Anabaptists that it is hard to imagine it being exceeded. Calvin, perhaps, gave it more theological justification in arguing for a fully disciplined church so that the wicked do not interfere with the faith of the community. He concludes his Catechism of the Church in Geneva with the stern warning that one of the tasks of the elders is "to bar from communion those whom they do not believe to be capable of receiving the Supper or to be able to be admitted without profaning the sacrament."[41] They would defile the eucharist for other believers. Therefore the community must be kept as pure as possible, always realizing that there are hypocrites but that the "true member of Christ" will approach with faith and repentance. By the end of the seventeenth century, Presbyterian sacramental seasons in Scotland concentrated on self-examination lest the community be profaned.

It cannot be said that the Church of England or the Puritans stressed this position any more than Anabaptists or Reformed. Communion fellowship in the bread and wine stands as one of the greatest rediscoveries of the Continental Reformation. The covenant theology of the New England Puritans simply reinforced what was already there. The Wesley hymns warmly rejoice in the same "sweet accord, / . . . / Then only can it closer be, / When all are join'd above." "Our perfect harmony" is received in the eucharist.[42]

This Reformation and early church legacy has certainly been welcomed in the churches of today. *Baptism, Eucharist and Ministry* speaks of "The Eucharist as Communion of the Faithful," claiming that "it is in the eucharist that the community of God's people is fully manifested. Eucharistic celebrations always have to do with the whole Church, and the whole Church is involved in each local eucharistic celebration."[43]

In many ways, these concepts are embodied in the new eucharistic rites. In the United Methodist rite, both minister and congregation declare to each other God's forgiveness "in the name of Jesus Christ." This leads to the Peace as a sign "of reconciliation and love." The eucharistic prayer concludes: "By your Spirit make us one with Christ, / one with each other, / and one in ministry to all the world."[44] Most Protestant liturgies now have the sign of the Peace, usually just before the offering. In the Episcopal Church, like the United Methodist

Church, the peace comes as an enacted reconciliation just after the confession of "our sins against God and our neighbor." Eucharistic Prayer C prays "make us one body, one spirit in Christ,"[45] and Prayer D specifies "union" with "Mary, with patriarchs, prophets, apostles, and martyrs . . . and all the saints."[46]

The Lutherans place the Peace before the offering or after the Lord's Prayer, the traditional Roman Catholic location. One eucharistic prayer prays that the communicants "may be united in the fellowship of the Holy Spirit."[47] A Presbyterian wording is "By your Spirit make us one with Christ, / that we may be one with all who share this feast, / united in ministry in every place."[48] Various other eucharistic prayers stress the sense of oneness with Christ and with each other, for we also are "in communion with all the faithful in heaven and on earth."[49] The sense of communion fellowship is inescapable in its expression in most recent Protestant eucharistic rites.

THE EUCHARIST AS SACRIFICE

The concept of sacrifice appears in a variety of forms in modern society. It is trivialized in newspaper ads for reduced-price sales. Even theologians treat it gingerly. *Baptism, Eucharist and Ministry* avoids mention of it other than in the phrases "sacrifice of praise" and "unique sacrifice of Christ,"[50] not wishing to cross that particular minefield of controversy. It is certainly the most disparate element in the new eucharistic rites.

Yet the concept of the eucharist as sacrifice has a long and very ancient history. Even the accounts of the Last Supper are filled with sacrificial language: "This is my blood of the [new] covenant" (Matt. 26:28). Hebrews is replete with sacrificial language and the first-century *Didache* (14:3) applies Malachi 1:11 to the eucharist as a "pure sacrifice" *(thusian)*. *First Clement* (36:1, 40:2, 4), also a first-century text, speaks repeatedly of offerings *(prosphoràs)*.

In the medieval West, the concept of the eucharist as sacrifice was of major importance, and sacrificial language was prominent in the canon of the mass. Medieval piety focused on the mass as a propitiatory sacrifice by which humans could find favor with God. The eucharist became the means by which humans appropriated the payment by Christ on our behalf. And thus evolved a whole system, well advanced by the late Middle Ages, of paying for masses to be said for the benefit of one's self and friends. At the crudest, it was God's grace being marketed.

It should surprise no one that Luther reserves his strongest condemnation of eucharistic corruptions for sacrifice. He calls it "by far the most wicked abuse of all . . . that the mass is a good work and a sacrifice." "The holy sacrament," he says, "has been turned into mere merchandise, a market, and a profit-making business."[51] If the first rule of politics is "don't hit their hustle," their finances, then Luther was wading into inevitable conflict by criticizing the crux of church finances. But beyond his shock at the financial abuses involved was his clear belief that the eucharist is a testament, a gift, a promise from God and not a human object. The medieval church, he argued, had made the mass into an offering from humans to God rather than God's free gift. Luther's most drastic liturgical step was in removing most of the canon of the mass as reeking of sacrifice.

It would be repetitive to quote the other reformers, virtually all of whom agreed completely with Luther in denying that the mass is a sacrifice. A new argument soon developed that to make the mass a sacrifice detracts from the sole sufficiency of Calvary, the sacrifice of Christ having long been equated with his death. The choice was clear for Calvin: "We shall have to confess either that Christ's sacrifice, which he fulfilled upon the cross, lacked the power to cleanse eternally, or that Christ had carried out one sacrifice, once for all, unto all ages."[52]

This became liturgical language for over four hundred years for Anglicans and Methodists in the opening words of the eucharistic prayer of 1549: "Who made there (by his one oblation once offered) a full, perfect, and sufficient sacrifice, oblation, and satisfaction, for the sins of the whole world." This is about as polemical as prayer can get. Cranmer did, however, acknowledge connections between the eucharist and sacrifice on three levels, largely because of biblical passages. The eucharist is a memorial of Christ's sacrifice, it is a "Sacrifice of praise and thanksgiving" (cf. Heb. 13:15), and "we offer and present unto thee (O Lord) our self, our souls, and bodies, to be a reasonable, holy, and lively sacrifice unto thee" (cf. Rom. 12:1). But Cranmer recoils from the thought that the eucharist is a good work offered to God.[53]

It is a surprise, then, to find the concept of the eucharist as sacrifice rise to such prominence in the work of the Wesleys, but it must be remembered that John Wesley was a patristics scholar and familiar with early references to the eucharist as sacrifice. Twelve of the *Hymns for the Lord's Supper* are in section 4, "The Holy Eucharist as it implies a Sacrifice." Many of the hymns were influenced by a seventeenth-century Anglican, Dr. Daniel Brevint, Dean of Lincoln. In his 1673 treatise *The Christian Sacrament and Sacrifice*, Brevint speaks of the eucharist as a memorial which "becomes a kind of *Sacrifice*, whereby we present before God the Father that precious Oblation of His Son once offered."[54] Thus the Wesleys can sing, "Victim Divine, Thy grace we claim / While thus Thy precious death we show"[55] or again, "Memorial of Thy sacrifice, / This Eucharistic mystery. . . ."[56]

Such a positive approach to the eucharist as mystery enabled United Methodist revisers to include the strongest positive statement of the eucharist as sacrifice in any current Protestant liturgy, a notion which reflects both Wesley and Augustine:

> In remembrance of these your mighty acts in Jesus Christ,
> we offer ourselves in praise and thanksgiving
> as a holy and living sacrifice,
> in union with Christ's offering for us.[57]

The Episcopal prayers are content to speak only of "this sacrifice of praise and thanksgiving" or of the partakers becoming "a living sacrifice in Christ."[58] This was far too much for Lutherans, and even in translating the *Apostolic Tradition, offerimus* was rendered as "we lift."[59] It therefore took some courage for the Presbyterian revisers to make a number of allusions to sacrifice in their eucharistic prayers. Phrases such as "accept this our sacrifice of praise and thanksgiving," "to be a living and holy sacrifice," "we claim his eternal sacrifice," and "memorial of his death and sacrifice," give various images of eucharistic sacrifice.[60] This gives hope that the ancient concept of the eucharist as a sacrifice, with sufficient safeguards, can still continue to be meaningful today.

THE EUCHARIST AS THE WORK OF THE HOLY SPIRIT

The Holy Spirit is not explicitly mentioned in the New Testament in the context of the eucharist. But this association soon appears in various locations in the early Christian period. In the *Apostolic Tradition*

(c. 217), God is invoked to "send your Holy Spirit upon the offering of your holy Church."[61] In the fourth century, Cyril of Jerusalem tells us the church does "call upon the merciful God to send forth His Holy Spirit upon the gifts lying before Him; that He may make the Bread the Body of Christ, and the Wine the Blood of Christ; for whatsoever the Holy Ghost has touched is sanctified and changed [metabebletai]."[62] In this development, the Holy Spirit has become operative for accomplishing the consecration. In similar language, the epiclesis, or invocation of the Spirit, in the Liturgy of St. John Chrysostom, the leading rite of the Orthodox and Eastern Catholic churches, reads: "send down your Holy Spirit on us and on these gifts set forth; and make this bread the precious body of your Christ, changing it by your Holy Spirit."[63]

The West went a different direction in attributing the consecration to the priest saying the words of Christ. The result is that, except at Pentecost, the Holy Spirit played a minor role in the Western mass. For a thousand years, the Holy Spirit was marginalized in the eucharistic consciousness of the West, simply being rattled off in doxological formulas pro forma. Luther is too much a child of his age drastically to alter this.

But in Zwingli we begin to find hints of the Holy Spirit as operative in presenting Christ to the communicants at the eucharist. The Holy Spirit operates to present Christ to us as faith: "only the Holy Spirit can give that faith which is trust in God."[64]

If this is an oblique connection, Calvin makes it head-on. He rescues from obscurity the work of the Holy Spirit, and it plays a major role in making us partakers of Christ's substance in heaven. "He [Christ] accomplishes this by the miraculous and secret virtue of his Spirit, for whom it is not difficult to associate things that are otherwise separated by an interval of space."[65] "It is through his [the Holy Spirit's] incomprehensible power that we come to partake of Christ's flesh and blood. . . . The secret power of the Spirit is the bond of our union with Christ."[66] There can be no doubt that the work of the Spirit is essential in Calvin's concept of the eucharist. It is, consequently, all the more amazing that there is so little mention of the Holy Spirit in Calvin's eucharistic rite. It does appear in the prayer for illumination, before the reading of the Word, which would occur in any Sunday service, eucharistic or not. The wording might be: "strengthen us now by thy Holy Spirit . . . so that we may hear and receive that same Word."[67] One would expect more, much more.

Cranmer's first eucharist does have a brief epiclesis, beseeching God, "With thy holy spirit and word, vouchsafe to bless and sanctify these thy gifts."[68] This disappeared in 1552 and has been missing ever since in English prayer books. But through the Episcopal Church of Scotland, the phrase "vouchsafe to bless and sanctify, with thy Word and Holy Spirit, these thy gifts" returned in American prayer books in 1789 and has been present ever since in similar words.

Wesley's *Sunday Service* makes no advances in this direction, but the eucharistic hymns have more than their share of references to the work of the Holy Spirit. One begins:

> Come, Holy Ghost, Thine influence shed,
>   And realize the sign;
> Thy life infuse into the bread,
> Thy power into the wine.[69]

The role shifts somewhat in another:

> Come, Thou everlasting Spirit,
>   Bring to every thankful mind
> All the Saviour's dying merit,
>
> . . . .
> . . . Remembrancer Divine.[70]

A similar function appears in another:

> Come, Holy Ghost, set to Thy seal,
> Thine inward witness give.[71]

The Spirit both transforms the gifts and the worshipers.

The Pentecostals did not need to be taught these lessons; they were experiencing them for themselves. Their worship was pervaded by signs of the Spirit's presence, bearing gifts which were dramatically exhibited in healings and speaking in tongues. They did not dispense with the outward signs as had the Quakers. But the eucharistic portion of many Pentecostal services often seems rushed and insignificant compared to the other miracles transpiring.

At any rate, the mainline churches have welcomed the warm presence of the Holy Spirit in virtually all the new eucharistic rites. *Baptism, Eucharist and Ministry,* following a trinitarian pattern, places

"The Eucharist as Invocation of the Spirit" third. It recognizes "the role of the Holy Spirit as that of the One who makes the historical words of Jesus present and alive" and makes "the bread and wine become the sacramental signs of Christ's body and blood." Furthermore, the "whole action of the eucharist" is "epikletic" since it all "depends upon the work of the Holy Spirit."[72]

Virtually all new eucharistic rites, Protestant or Roman Catholic, contain a distinct epiclesis in their eucharistic prayers. The Methodist tradition picked up from the Reformed tradition a prayer for illumination before the reading of the Word. By reverse borrowing, the new United Methodist version now appears as the first option in the Presbyterian rite. In the eucharistic prayer, the United Methodist epiclesis begins: "Pour out your Holy Spirit on us gathered here, / and on these gifts of bread and wine."[73] Various forms appear in the Episcopal rites: "Sanctify them by your Holy Spirit" or "send your Holy Spirit" or "your Holy Spirit may descend upon us, and upon these gifts."[74] One Lutheran version says "Send now, we pray, your Holy Spirit, the spirit of our Lord and of his resurrection," and another text has a congregational response: "Amen. Come, Holy Spirit."[75] As one might expect, the Presbyterian prayers rectify what was missing in Calvin's rite with words such as "pour out your Holy Spirit upon us / and upon these your gifts of bread and wine" or "by your Holy Spirit bless and make holy / both us and these your gifts of bread and wine" or "let your Holy Spirit move in power over us / and over these earthly gifts of bread and wine" or "your Holy Spirit may descend upon us, and upon these gifts, / sanctifying them / and showing them to be holy gifts for your holy people."[76]

What the West ignored for so many centuries has now been recognized and restored to its rightful role.[77]

THE EUCHARIST AND SOCIAL JUSTICE

Much has been written in our time about the eucharist and social justice. But before the work of F. D. Maurice in the nineteenth century, this would have appeared an odd topic to all Christians. The Quakers were an exception of course, for they had recognized the strong connection between worship and social justice as early as the seventeenth century and this had changed their attitudes on many issues. It is because of their worship that they began the first crusades against slavery and that the leaders of the Woman's Rights Convention in 1848, with the exception of Elizabeth Cady Stanton, were all Quakers. But their worship did not involve an outward and visible eucharist.

There is much ambiguity here, for we now recognize that the eucharist can be a major source of injustice, too, especially if it marginalizes people.[78] Those whose full human value is denied by the eucharist may experience it as oppressive. This may be the case for women, children, and minorities. It is for both ethical and theological reasons that the question of the eucharist for children has become such a pressing issue for the pedobaptist churches. The same applies to those with mental disabilities. Does our worth depend on our cognitive abilities? Should women be barred from presiding? Does racism determine whom we choose for leadership roles? Can we eat together while one group continues to oppress another? All these questions have been seriously discussed in recent years.

The positive approach, of course, is that the eucharist meets us all as equals before God. We come to church to meet our God and the first thing that happens is that we meet our neighbor. On the way to communion is the only time we pass all segments of our society. There is a fine equality at the Lord's table as we all go to receive Christ. It is a gift, no matter who we are. But we must not forget the hungry elsewhere.

The eucharist also allies us with all of humanity, indeed all of creation. As the United Methodist rite says in addressing God, "You have given yourself to us. / Grant that we may . . . give ourselves for others."[79] It welcomes us to "ministry to all the world" on the basis of Christ's self giving on our behalf. Because we have received, we can give. The service of worship leads to the service of humanity. The local church relates to the universal church, which relates to all of humanity. The eucharist proclaims this relatedness each time.

It also relates us to the natural universe. At the heart of the eucharist are material elements, bread and wine. We are not trying to be more spiritual than God in ignoring God's creation. We acknowledge that we have a responsibility for the material world as well as the spiritual. Our encounter with Christ in the eucharist is also an encounter with Christ in the political, social, and economic areas of life.

Now that we have once again included creation as part of the work of God for which we give thanks, we realize how responsible we are to be stewards of the natural world. Bread and wine remind us how dependent we are on the fertility of nature and on the work of other humans. We are reminded of our stewardship for God's creation in receiving Christ through the very physical elements of the created world.

Fortunately, the new eucharistic rites remind us of our ongoing responsibilities to our neighbor and to the created world. Our most spiritual act is also our most worldly.

CHAPTER SIX

Commonly Called Sacraments

The Reformation narrowed the number of sign-acts that could be called sacraments, just as the thirteenth century also had in selecting seven instead of an undetermined number. But in neither case did that mean that the rites and ceremonies not designated as sacraments disappeared. The rite of religious profession still survived even if the latter scholastics no longer considered it a sacrament. Such rites as penance, the healing of the sick, Christian marriage, ordination, and Christian burial obviously served important functions within the life of Protestant communities, just as they had before the Reformation. But they were not considered as instituted by Christ in scripture and hence no longer were called sacraments.

One can question whether this distinction made much difference to the average worshiper. It did in the sense that baptism and the Lord's Supper were regarded as obligatory on the basis of divine command, whereas extreme unction or penance could quietly fade away or become transmuted in various ways. And marriage and Christian burial could be secularized and pushed outside the church doors at different times and places. Defining only two actions as sacraments also meant that their form and matter were fixed with more certainty whereas other acts could be more fluid and evolve on their own.

It is also instructive what new rites did not develop. With the Reformers' emphasis on the sanctity of any useful vocation, it is strange that no rites for entering a vocation evolved. The stress on reading the Scriptures pushed education into new prominence and shaped confirmation or public profession of faith into something resembling graduation exercises. Much of this has already been discussed under baptismal practices. We shall not repeat our consideration of confirmation here, although the Anglican Articles of Religion list confirmation as one of the five "commonly called Sacraments."

Several actions, such as marriage and caring for the dead, are common to all humanity, whether Christian or not. We can refer to them as "natural sacraments." Others, such as penance and healing, are referred to in the Acts of the Apostles (Acts 2:38; 16:18, etc.) and elsewhere in the epistles (James 5:14-16; Heb. 6:4, etc.). So we may speak of them as "apostolic sacraments."[1] Confirmation we shall regard as part of baptism, misplaced by a series of historical accidents. The Lord's Supper and baptism we can refer to as "gospel sacraments," beginning with the Last Supper and the baptism of Jesus.

Not all of these natural or apostolic sacraments have been pursued with equal vigor in the nearly five centuries of Protestantism. But there are strong indications that today each of them is receiving fresh attention. We shall make a quick survey of how Protestants at various times and places have prioritized or neglected penance, the healing of the sick, Christian marriage, ordination, and Christian burial. In each case, changing practices, controversies, and meanings have surfaced over the past five centuries. This should suggest the basically sacramental nature of each and help raise the question of whether either the thirteenth or the sixteenth century was justified in limiting the number of actions called sacraments. Perhaps the first twelve Christian centuries were right in keeping the number open.

PENANCE, CONFESSION, OR RECONCILIATION

By definition, all Christians are sinners, falling far short of the perfection the Gospels urge. So the Christian life is a recurring process of reconciliation with God and neighbor, usually through same acts of confession and pardon. The church has had to deal with these realities ever since its beginnings (Heb. 6:4). By a long process, moving from public penance before the whole community for notorious sinners only, penance became a private act expected of everyone of the age of reason. The Fourth Lateran Council of 1215 mandated annual confession, and the minimum often became the norm. "Late medieval penance, then, stressed the therapeutic element, purification, to remove sin and eliminate the debt of eternal punishment incurred by mortal sin. . . . Other means, indulgences in particular, were necessary to deal with the temporal punishment due to sin."[2] The priest alone possessed the power of the keys to retain or to remit sin, for the community no longer functioned in penance.

Luther's initial outburst of anger was directed to the sale of indulgences as vitiating the orderly care of souls through penance. He was concerned to reform penance, not abolish it. In 1519 he could say, "There is no greater sin than not to believe this article of 'the forgiveness of sins' which we pray daily in the Creed."[3] God's word acts in absolution to comfort and strengthen sinners. Luther is willing at first to call penance a sacrament in his *Babylonian Captivity* because of its "word of divine promise."[4] Despite abuses, Luther wished to retain penance: "As to the current practice of private confession, I am heartily in favor of it, . . . and I would not have it abolished."[5] Luther's most radical statement is that "Christ has given to every one of his believers the power to absolve even open sins,"[6] thereby breaking every clerical monopoly of the sacrament.

Penance plays an important role in Luther's catechisms. One may confess one's sins to "God alone or to our neighbor." But Luther also provided a "A Short Order of Confession Before the Priest for the Common Man" in the 1529 edition of the Small Catechism and later revised it in 1531. It takes the form of a general confession of sin with particular details confessed, if necessary. In 1531, the "father confessor" pronounces that "I, by the command of Jesus Christ our Lord, forgive thee all thy sin."[7] Absent is a cataloging by species and number of sinful acts. But it is a definite act of confession and absolution of a penitent before a priest. It was certainly Luther's intention that penance be continued as an important act of reassuring the sinner of God's forgiveness.[8]

Much less of this survived than Luther wished. There was a revival of this practice in nineteenth-century Germany under Pastor Wilhelm Loehe,[9] with a visit to the pastor necessary before each communion. A remnant has survived today in the Lutheran practice of notifying the pastor before receiving communion. But Luther's expectation that penance would play a major role in pastoral life had a rather short history.

In a way that Luther did not expect, and probably did not relish, the Anabaptists developed a strong force for the discipline of their communities by the use of the ban. According to the Schleitheim Confession of 1527, the ban is employed for those who "somehow slip and fall into error and sin, being inadvertently overtaken. The same [shall] be warned twice privately and the third time be publicly admonished before the entire congregation according to the command of Christ."[10] Matthew 18:15-17 was their source, as well as 1 Corinthians 5:11-13. The whole purpose was that a pure gathering could share in communion together.

But the power of the keys, which all the baptized exercised, was meant to heal. As Menno Simons wrote, "we do not want to expel any, but rather to receive; not to amputate, but rather to heal; not to discard, but rather to win back; not to grieve, but rather to comfort; not to condemn, but rather to save."[11] But he was also aware that "one scabby sheep mars the whole flock."[12] Debates raged over how severe the shunning of the person banned should be, whether it could even divide husband and wife, and whether "the commandment regarding marriage" was stronger than that about shunning.

Some Anabaptists developed a sign-act of reconciliation or readmission. This was not unlike the reconciliation of penitents in the early church and in effect was a renewal of baptism. "So also after he fell," Peter Riedeman counseled, when one "was separated from the church he must likewise be received by a sign, that is through the laying on of hands, which must be done by a servant of the gospel. This indicates that he once more has part and is rooted in the grace of God."[13] The minister by a tangible sign-act effected reconciliation with the community.

These forms of penance endure partly because of the small, disciplined, sectarian nature of Mennonite, Amish, and Hutterite communities. Whether this discipline could have succeeded in larger church-type communities is a good question, although the New England Puritan community made the experiment. *The Scarlet Letter* is not all fiction.

For most of the Reformed Tradition, another course opened up. The Fourth Lateran Council of 1215 had linked confession to the eucharist, a fateful move. The late medieval eucharist had become increasingly penitential, laden with apologies for one's unworthiness. The Reformed Tradition took this even further, making each eucharist a fresh occasion for examination of conscience and a dose of introspection. The prevailing eucharistic piety of the late Middle Ages was enshrined in Reformed liturgies down to the present. It is significant that the Presbyterian eucharist still mandates general confession and pardon as part of the Gathering rite. The eucharist is always prefaced by confession.

More than anyone else, Martin Bucer led the way. His eucharistic rite published in Strasbourg in 1539 begins with three possible confessions. The most impressive of these is based on a paraphrase of the Ten Commandments. One confesses that "I have sinned in manifold ways against thee and thy commandments" and then examines all kinds of possibilities.[14] Calvin's rite begins with the confession that "we are . . . born in iniquity and corruption, prone to do evil, incapable of any good, and that in our depravity we transgress thy holy commandments without end or ceasing."[15] As if that were not enough, the congregation then sings the first table of the Commandments.

The Decalogue was to have an even more lasting incarnation as part of the eucharist. It began with the Anglican prayer book of 1552 and lasted to the present in the English prayer book and until 1965 in the American Methodist eucharist, although in 1935 the Beatitudes became an option instead. The same instinct reached its culmination in the Scottish sacramental seasons of the late seventeenth century, in which once each year the eucharist provided a several-day occasion of self-examination and preparation.

The consequence was that for most Protestants, penance became subsumed in a penitential eucharist. The eucharist became, as the Methodist rite of 1939 said, a time to "ask God's mercy for their transgressions in times past and grace to keep the law in time to come."[16] In such a fashion, the eucharist remained a somber reminder of Good Friday. In Dutch churches, the eucharist was always celebrated on Good Friday, and people wore their funeral clothes. Penance did not disappear, it simply attached itself to the eucharist.

In the hands of John Wesley, a new form of penance appeared in the group discipline of class meetings. Here spiritual direction was performed in a corporate fashion, based on James 5:16: "Confess your sins to one another, and pray for one another, so that you may be healed." This involved weekly meetings for those who had affirmed such questions as "Do you desire to be told of all your faults, and that plain and home?" Each week they would be asked: "What known sins have you committed since our last meeting?"[17] It was a stringent discipline, and it worked well for over a century until Methodism expanded into a church. This form of "Christian conference" made penance a group process.

In the Catholic Revival in the Church of England in the nineteenth century, a major effort was made to revive private confession to a priest, or "auricular confession," as it was known. This aroused stubborn opposition as a betrayal of the Reformation and led to salacious imaginations about priests hearing the confessions of women. The title of a tract tells it all: "The House of Lords on Ritualism in the Church, Confession & Absolution: Shocking Disclosures."[18] One of the reasons given for advancing confession to a priest was that both of Cranmer's rites for the Visitation of the Sick had invited confession by the sick person. But to many Victorians, it appeared a strange and dangerous practice.

What took its place, instead, for most Protestants was a ministry of counseling. That had a long precedent, such as the advice in Richard Baxter's *The Reformed Pastor*, which advocated visiting from house to house to examine the state of parishioners' souls.[19] In the twentieth century, new psychological insights made counseling both a spiritual discipline and a form of therapy. It was meant to heal more than to chasten. At times, a view of psychological professionalism tended to dominate; at others counseling took the form of spiritual direction.

In recent years, the possibilities of corporate services of confession have been discussed but rarely acted on. As Reinhold Niebuhr pointed out, we are often willing to sin as a group by doing acts we would abhor as individuals, as in war. United Methodists so far have not published official services of corporate repentance which could serve in times of national turmoil over racism, sexism, war, and other forms of corporate guilt. The Episcopal Church has an individual office for "Reconciliation of a Penitent" but not yet a corporate office of reconciliation.[20] Lutherans have a "Brief Order for Confession and Forgiveness" often used as a preface to the eucharist, but its emphasis is almost entirely on individual sin.[21] Presbyterians have produced "A Service of Repentance and Forgiveness for Use with a Penitent Individual," meant to be used in private.[22]

Certainly sin is alive and well, and various forms of relieving the soul of its burden are practiced in private. But relatively little has been done so far in providing corporate forms for confessing corporate sins. Maybe these will come in the next stage of liturgical revision.

HEALING THE SICK

At first glance, healing may not seem the focus of the tradition inherited in what had come to be known as extreme unction, a term coined by Peter Lombard in the middle of the twelfth century. The late medieval consensus had made it a sacrament of the dying. Charles Gusmer summarizes this development from a sacrament of healing to one for the dying: by the late Middle Ages, "the proper time for the sacrament is *in extremis*, in the agony of death, because the recipient is unable to sin further and thus cannot negate the effect of the sacrament."[23] It had become a final opportunity to obtain remission of sins, a kind of eternal fire insurance.

As might be expected, Luther states firmly that unction is not a sacrament. He picked up on the tradition that it was instituted by James (James 5:14-15) and denied that any "apostle has the right on his own authority to institute a sacrament."[24] Furthermore, James 5 speaks of healing, not dying. On the other hand, Luther would approve of "prayer . . . made . . . in full faith by older, graver, and saintly men," so that "as many as we wished would be healed."[25] He interprets the *presbytérous* of James 5:14 as elders, the purpose as health, and the means as faith. Near the end of his own life, Luther returned to the James 5 passage in suggesting ministering to the sick by "two or three good men . . . the pastor . . . anointing, imposing hands, . . . saying the Creed and Lord's Prayer . . . three times in one day," plus public prayer.[26]

Calvin is characteristically blunt: in opposition to the apostle James, "these fellows smear with their grease not the sick but half-dead corpses when they are already drawing their last breath." They have also distorted presbyter to mean only priests.[27] The witness of fifth-century Pope Innocent I that all Christians could anoint, however, did not lead Calvin to reinstitute the practice. But ministry to the sick remained an important pastoral responsibility. Calvin clearly expected pastoral visitation of the sick in his service book, while leaving the form free for the pastor.[28] And he announced in a letter of 1558 that "the supper is not administered to the sick, [which] is displeasing to me." Forces in Geneva had made it impossible "without great contention."[29] Calvin lost a few!

A more explicit approach appears in the first *Book of Common Prayer* of 1549, in "The Order for the Visitation of the Sick." It contains prayers to "restore unto this sick person his former health" but accepts that God may will otherwise. The theology we may find troubling; it attributes sickness to "Gods visitation" whether it "be to try your patience," or "to correct and amend" the afflicted. Sickness is "the chastisement of the Lord."[30] The sick person is first examined according to faith and morals and then led to confession, culminating in an absolution which reappeared in nineteenth-century confessions. Then, if the sick person desires, there is anointing with oil. The rite is followed by "The Communion of the Sick" which provides for bringing the bread and wine from the eucharist, if it be celebrated that day, to the sick person. Otherwise, a brief eucharistic rite is provided for the sickroom. In the case that the sick person cannot receive physically, "he doth eat and drink spiritually."[31]

In the 1552 prayer book, the anointing has disappeared altogether. And the communion is no longer brought from the church; the eucharist is celebrated entirely in the sick room so all present may hear the Word.

The Puritans took visitation of the sick very seriously as a pastoral opportunity to instruct the patient so as "to make a sanctified use of Gods Visitation, neither despising his chastening, nor waxing weary of his correction."[32] Outlines of prayers are provided, including those for recovery "that he may glorify God in the remaining part of his life."[33] But assurances of pardon are also to be offered, that the dying "may behold Death without fear." And friends and relatives are exhorted "to consider their own mortality."

John Wesley retained "The Communion of the Sick" with provision for an abbreviated sickroom celebration.[34] Many early English Methodists crowded into sickroom celebrations simply to have the opportunity to receive communion.

In the early eighteenth century, a group of German pietists, often referred to as Dunkards because of their insistence on immersion of adults, began practicing anointing of the sick. In modern times, as the Church of the Brethren or the Brethren Church, they have continued the practice of anointing the sick on the basis of scripture (Mark 6:13, James 5:14-15). A recent rite of the Church of the Brethren provides for anointing with oil three times "for the forgiveness of your sins, / for the strengthening of your faith, / and for the restoration of wholeness in your body according to the will of God."[35]

For the most part, healing became a ministry specialized in by non-mainline groups in the nineteenth century. Mary Baker Eddy founded the Church of Christ, Scientist in 1879 to proclaim the unreality of sickness and other forms of evil and to minister by making sufferers aware of the reality of God's loving power. Another woman, Ellen G. White, led the way in organizing the Seventh-Day Adventist Church, which placed a heavy emphasis on health reform and founded many hospitals.

Healing really came into its own in the Pentecostal Tradition, where the apostolic gift of healing frequently appeared as one of the gifts of the Holy Spirit. Various leaders, such as Aimee Semple MacPherson, possessed healing gifts, but many other Pentecostals came to give evidence of healing ministries. Frequently, services include an act of healing with sufferers invited to come forward to receive the laying on of hands and occasionally anointing. Often, it is not the minister but lay members who have the gift of healing. Many of the new and rapidly growing independent churches of Africa are structured around a charismatic healer.

After ignoring for so long a ministry of healing and regarding it as often being bizarre, the mainline Protestant churches have begun to appropriate this ministry. In several cases, the biggest additions to the new service books revolve around healing services. These additions have produced little controversy, but the changes are very significant.

A major shift for United Methodists is the addition of a chapter entitled "Healing Services and Prayers" in the 1992 *Book of Worship* whereas its predecessors had none. The first service is a complete order of worship, including a special eucharistic prayer for this rite, communion, anointing with oil, and/or the laying on of hands. Another order follows for use in private but with similar components. Somewhat controversial was "A Service of Hope After Loss of Pregnancy" or, alternatively, "A Service of Death and Resurrection for a Stillborn Child." And there are forms for ministry with persons "Going Through Divorce," "Suffering from Addiction or Substance Abuse," "with Aids," "with Life-Threatening Illness," or "in Coma or Unable to Communicate."[36]

The Episcopal prayer book of 1979 contains a greatly expanded "Ministration to the Sick," which can be used as a public service or in private. Laying on of hands and anointing are provided as well as communion. *The Book of Occasional Services* of 1979 added a full rite of "A Public Service of Healing," and even dared to mention (very cautiously) exorcism. The "Public Service of Healing" contains a "Litany of Healing" and various appropriate prayers.[37]

The Lutheran rites appear in *Occasional Services* (1982) as "Service of the Word for Healing" and "Laying on of Hands and Anointing the Sick."[38] The first is intended to be public, the second private. Both contain the possibility of laying on of hands and anointing.

A major step forward for Presbyterians was the publication in 1990 of *Services for Occasions of Pastoral Care*.[39] These all appeared in the 1993 *Book of Common Worship* as both private and public services "for wholeness." Both include the possibility of laying on of hands, anointing with oil, and holy communion. Sickroom communion is also provided for.[40]

These new rites give evidence of a major reappropriation of the church's ministry of healing. The fears of the Reformation era have been shed. Although it is difficult to tell how widely the new rites are used, the new healing services are available and have produced very little controversy so far for such radical changes.

CHRISTIAN MARRIAGE

There is a fine ambiguity in weddings. For not only are they celebrated in all cultures, Christian or not, but for most of Christian history they were not even performed in churches. It was a long and slow process in moving weddings from the home or tavern to the church. By Chaucer's time in the fourteenth century, weddings had finally arrived at the church's door where other legal contracts were performed. His Wife of Bath had had "five husbands at the church door" and was looking for number six. Even Luther's rite of 1529 had gone no further; it provides for his Hans and Greta to exchange vows at the entrance to the church before proceeding inside for the reading of scripture and the blessing.[41] Luther's own custom was to add a wedding sermon, delineating the duties of the partners.

Luther had spewed forth his usual denunciation of marriage as a sacrament. Furthermore, he said, it had been enshrouded by so vast a complex of canon law as to need liberation. Luther abhorred divorce, even preferring bigamy which, at least, had its biblical precedents. Luther added to the wedding service Matthew 19:6, "What God hath joined." For Luther, marriage was a thousand times more holy than monastic vows. He made the transition himself in 1525, marrying a Cistercian nun. For many of his contemporary priests, marriage was the clear sign of their joining the Reformation.

Luther had a high view of marriage, as expressed in his treatise of 1522 *The Estate of Marriage*.[42] At the same time, it was not a sacrament but a secular matter, so the civil authorities could regulate it. In one sense he is merely conservative, since the church for most of its history had adopted a rather diffident attitude and allowed local customs to prevail. Still, Luther was opening the possibility of marriage as a purely secular estate.

The Anabaptists frequently required converts to be remarried or "retrothed" because they had entered a new realm of being through faith and baptism. This had changed all relationships. Thus it was a divisive issue whether the shunning of those banned should separate husband and wife at bed and board.

Calvin was colorful in denying that marriage was a sacrament. "Farming, building, cobbling, and barbering are lawful ordinances of God, and yet are not sacraments"; marriage was no more a sacrament than those.[43] He was aware of the translator's mistake in translating *mystérion* in Ephesians 5:32 as *sacramentum*, on which much of the argument that marriage was a sacrament had depended. Nevertheless, Calvin had a high esteem for marriage and took that step himself in 1540. In 1542, he published a marriage rite in his service book *The Form of Prayers*, a light revision of his 1540 rite for Strasbourg, and like it heavily dependent upon William Farel's 1533 rite, which Calvin had inherited in Geneva.[44] Calvin's rite as published seems heavily didactic with stress that marriage began in paradise by God's ordinance and has ample New Testament warrant. The vows are taken after inquiry of the congregation about impediments. His vows are prefaced by a most explicit statement about the obligations of each partner. But no mention of the ring appears. Then there is a reading from Matthew 19 with a short exhortation to live together in holiness,[45] then a prayer and a blessing. Much of this rite was followed by John Knox in his *Form of Prayers* of 1556, later used by the Church of Scotland.[46]

Marriage rites have a tendency to be the most conservative because so much of social value is at stake. It is not surprising that the Church of England rite should be largely taken over from the Sarum rite then in use in Southern England. The promise to be "Bonere and buxum" disappeared from the bride's vows and the husband no longer takes her "for fairer for fouler" as in some medieval rites. Still, it seems strange that the medieval priorities for marriage are reiterated in an exhortation: first, procreation; second, "to avoid fornication"; and only third, "for the mutual society, help, and comfort."[47] The betrothal and espousal vows had already been in English for at least two hundred years and were only slightly altered. A wonderful phrase appears in the ring ceremony: "with my body I thee worship."[48] The concluding rubric reads, "The new married persons (the same day of their marriage) must receive the holy communion."[49] The giving of gold or silver with the rings disappeared in 1552, but most of the rite survived intact.

The Puritans mandated the publishing of the banns. Weddings were to be celebrated in church but not on a Sunday for fear of frivolity profaning the sabbath. The vows emphasize that marriage is a covenant. The Puritans opposed the giving of rings as not warranted by scripture. The minister is to "pronounce them to be husband and wife" immediately after the vows and then conclude with a blessing. In 1653, the drastic step was taken, though soon reversed, of secularizing marriage altogether in the hands of justices of the peace.[50]

John Wesley's "Form of the Solemnization of Matrimony" is conservative in following the *Book of Common Prayer* except that he does away with the giving away of the bride and dispenses with the wedding ring.[51] Both of these were later replaced by American Methodists, but a significant change came as early as 1864, when the Methodist Episcopal Church removed from the bride's vows the words "and to obey."[52]

This stress on equality has permeated the new rites which, like Wesley, are reluctant to mention that the bride is given away or that there is any inequality present. Most have reworded the pronouncement to show that the couple actually perform the marriage themselves, as in the United Methodist "I announce to you that they are husband and wife."[53] A conscious effort has been made to make the new services explicitly for Christians and not just generic marriage. And further, they are intended to be genuine services of worship for a Christian congregation.

Whereas previous Methodist books discouraged the eucharist at weddings, this time around a eucharistic prayer is provided and rubrics encourage the possibility of communion. The traditional marriage rite is also provided plus the blessing of a civil marriage, a reaffirmation of the marriage covenant, and anniversary prayers.

The Episcopal rite adds vows of the congregation to uphold the marriage and gives the congregation the possibility of participation in the forms of hymnody, psalmody, and prayer. The Lutheran rite does not use the traditional English vows and has no betrothal vows. Luther's addition of Matthew 19:6 remains: "Those whom God has joined together let no one put asunder," one of the hardest phrases to make contemporary. The Presbyterian rite has yet another set of vows and the minister does "proclaim that they are now husband and wife."[54] A pattern is worked out for fitting the service into a normal Lord's Day service. There is also the possibility of the eucharist and a special eucharistic prayer.[55] An alternative blessing ceremony is provided "for Those Previously Married in a Civil Ceremony."[56]

A most encouraging sign was the development of *A Christian Celebration of Marriage: An Ecumenical Liturgy*, first published in 1985.[57] This is a compilation of the best elements of twenty-eight different English-speaking rites from around the world. It is not greatly different from any of the services already described, although the prayers make a special effort to remember all of humanity on this joyous occasion. By 1998, it had not been approved by Rome, although the American Catholic bishops have requested that approval. In many dioceses, the majority of marriages are interchurch unions, so such a service would have wide use. It is an eloquent testimony as to how much practice and meaning have coalesced among the churches on Christian marriage. The service also provides for direct cooperation by clergy of different churches. The vows of all the churches announce lifelong intent although the realities of life often intervene.

ORDINATION

In the medieval church, ordained ministry had come to be the principal source of power and authority within the church. The rites of ordination had evolved, largely by grafting onto the primitive core secondary elements symbolic of the conveyance of power. These included the handing over of instruments of the designated order (keys, book, chalice), anointing of hands, and vesting in clerical garb. Most parishes had a variety of ministries: minor orders such as porter, acolyte, exorcist, and lector plus several men in major orders of sub-deacon, deacon, and priest. As late as the twelfth century, Peter Lombard could state that bishops were of a different dignity and office, but not a different order.[58] Aquinas repeats this in the thirteenth century: "The episcopate is a dignity rather than an order."[59] Ordination to priesthood brought power to preside at the eucharist, hear confessions, and anoint the sick. Much of medieval church finances centered to a large extent on the power to say mass. Mass stipends supported large numbers of priests.

Luther's assault on the sacramental system denied that ordination was a sacrament: "It is an invention of the church of the pope. . . . There is not a single word said about it in the whole New Testament."[60] Any word of promise is lacking. Luther's radical conclusion is that "we are all equally priests, that is to say, we have the same power in respect to the Word and the sacraments."[61] He had expressed the same concept earlier in 1520 in his *Address to the Christian Nobility of the German Nation.*

But Luther's esteem for ordained ministry evolved, chiefly in the direction of seeing the chief function of pastors as being that of preachers of the Word. The hundreds of priests who joined the Reformation left Luther with a major task of teaching them to how to preach the gospel. His sermons were published as examples, the postils. In this light, ordained ministry came to have a high value for him because the preaching of the Word was essential for the life of the church.[62] Increasingly he saw the ordained ministry as a gift of God. As early as 1525, Luther found it necessary himself to ordain a pastor and eventually a bishop. In 1539, Luther published a form for "The Ordination of Ministers of the Word." It is a radical shift from the medieval rite with all its ceremonies. The climax has the presbyters laying hands on the heads of the ordinands while the ordaining pastor says the Lord's Prayer.[63]

Even the Anabaptists, radical as they were in so many ways, came to value an ordained ministry. They often would reordain priests who became their leaders, so drastic was the shift that a new baptism brought. Clergy leaders were usually called and ordained by a local group. Frequently they had all too short ministries, as many of the leaders were soon martyred. Women and children, too, joined the lists of martyrs.

As with everything else, Calvin is always systematic here. He hesitated on rejecting ordination as a sacrament, but did so because it was limited to so few.[64] Calvin proposed a fourfold ministry to include both clergy and laity, all based on what he took to be "four orders of office instituted by our Lord for the government of his Church. First, pastors; then doctors [teachers]; next elders; and fourth deacons." The pastor is minister of word and sacrament. The pastor is chosen by other ministers (presbyters), approved by the city council, and then ordained without the laying on of hands. Calvin recognized that this last act was biblical (Acts 6:6) but felt too many superstitions were intertwined with it.[65] Thus a tactile succession was lost for much of the Reformed tradition. The doctor was essentially a lecturer in theology and the Bible. The elders were laymen responsible for church discipline, "to have oversight of the life of everyone." In Geneva, this meant a dozen men who were replaced at regular intervals. The deacons, too, were laymen who had responsibility for the poor and sick. These patterns became the norm for the Reformed tradition, although pastor and doctor were frequently one and the same in small parishes.[66]

The Church of England was considerably more conservative in outward form. Cranmer's first ordinal appeared in 1550 and was revised two years later. The influence of Martin Bucer is paramount instead of the medieval pontifical. Cranmer retains a three-ordered ministry of deacon, priest, and bishop, the first two being ordained, the bishop being consecrated. Cranmer's "view that bishops and priests were one order was in line with the teaching of the other writings of the period and with the opinions of many medieval theologians."[67] Cranmer dispenses with most of the ceremonies inherited but makes the high point of the ordination of priests an imperative formula: "Receive the holy ghost" for the forgiveness or retention of sins and dispense "the word of god, and of his holy Sacraments."[68] Candidates for the diaconate must be "learned in the Latin tongue, and sufficiently instructed in holy Scripture" and behave so well "in this inferior office" that they may "be called unto the higher ministries."[69] Cranmer deliberately avoided much of the language of the medieval pontificals in ordaining priests to a sacrificial priesthood. Still, it is remarkable that he retained the term *priest* even in the 1552 eucharistic rite. The minor orders and the subdiaconate simply disappeared. Clergy were allowed to marry.

The Quakers took the most radical step of all. All members of a meeting ministered to each other without benefit of ordination. This has important consequences for Western culture. On the basis of what they experienced in their worship, they realized that the inner light or Holy Spirit could use anyone, regardless of sex, race, or servitude, to minister to the community. The Quakers became the first to crusade against slavery and for the equality of women. The Spirit does not discriminate so Christians should not either. Their vision of justice led to reforms in prisons and the treatment of the mentally ill.

Among the American Puritans, congregationalism prevailed. Each community called and ordained its own pastor. He was seen primarily as a scholar of God's Word and was distinguished from his flock mostly by his learning. The community that had called him also laid on hands, although neighboring preachers might be called in to preach the ordination sermon.[70]

John Wesley soon developed a system of lay preachers, including both men and women. But he was enough of a traditionalist to insist that ordination was necessary to baptize or to preside at the eucharist. His research as a patristics scholar convinced Wesley that historically priests and bishops were simply different job descriptions but the same order, a position held by other scholars such as Peter Lombard or Thomas Cranmer. Recent scholarship seems to reinforce the position that these were not distinct orders in the New Testament and early church. Wesley writes: Peter King's "account of the primitive church convinced me many years ago, that Bishops and Presbyters are the same order, and consequently have the same right to ordain."[71] The *Sunday Service* of 1784 contained rites for "ordaining" deacons, elders (presbyters), and "superintendants." Wesley's American followers quickly changed "superintendant" to bishop. American Methodist orders derive through Wesley from Bishop John Potter of Oxford (later, in 1737, Archbishop of Canterbury). Wesley takes the conservative approach: an ordained elder is necessary for the eucharist so therefore ordain more men.

The radical position evolved for the same purpose, so that Christians on the American frontier could have a weekly eucharist. The followers of Barton Stone and Alexander Campbell came together on the Kentucky frontier in 1831 in what is often called the Restoration Movement, which produced the Christian Church (Disciples of Christ) and the Churches of Christ. This was an era of Jacksonian democracy in politics and the Campbellites, as they were often called, succeeded in establishing liturgical democracy by calling lay elders to administer the Lord's Supper. Local communities chose senior men to preside at the Lord's table. Ordained clergy might preach and teach, but the Lord's table belonged to lay leaders. Mormons dealt with this by making most male members priests of a variety of priesthoods. The Plymouth Brethren likewise encouraged lay presiders. All of these groups—Methodists, Disciples, Mormons, Plymouth Brethren—were motivated by the desire for a weekly eucharist but came to opposite solutions with presiding done either by the ordained or nonordained.

A major step was taken in the second half of the nineteenth century with the move to the ordination of women, a process still underway. In 1853, the Congregational Church of South Butler, New York, took the radical step of ordaining Antoinette Louisa Brown (later Blackwell) as its minister. A hundred years later, in 1956, the Methodist Church gave women full ordination, and in 1980 Marjorie Matthews became the first woman bishop in historic continuity. Now a struggle is going on within the churches over the ordination of openly gay men and women. All would grant that the church has always ordained discrete homosexual men.

A different movement was gaining momentum in the Anglican communion because of the Catholic Revival. This grew out of resistance to an openly secular government bringing long overdue reforms in the (Anglican) Church of Ireland. The resistance led to emphasizing the distinctions between the ordained and the laity. Architecturally, this took the form of the reinstitution of roodscreens in churches, "exhibiting, what is so wholesome for both to remember, the distinction which must exist between the Clergy and their flocks."[72] Theologically, it led to claims for an unbroken tactile apostolic succession from the apostles down to the Anglican bishops. Recent scholarship would consider this highly dubious historically for any church. Much of this ecclesiastical triumphalism was dashed by the Roman Catholic encyclical *Apostolicae Curae* of Leo XIII in 1896, which concluded that Anglican orders were "absolutely null and utterly void," a fairly firm denunciation! It declared that there were defects in both the form of the ordination of priests in the 1552 *Book of Common Prayer* and the lack of intention to continue a sacrificial priesthood. We now know that the first objection would disqualify many early and medieval ordinations from being valid, and the concept of eucharistic sacrifice has shifted so greatly within Catholicism in recent years as to be problematic itself. But the document was reaffirmed in 1998 at a high level in Rome. The result is that officially

Roman Catholics reject the validity of Anglican orders and (by implication) eucharists, Anglicans reject Methodist orders, and Methodists are charitable to almost anyone!

The nature of ordained ministry has thus become the central theological issue in ecumenism. Some common threads are emerging, especially the emphasis on the ministry of all the baptized or the general ministry of the church. Discussions continue on how the ministry of the ordained or representative ministry of the church relates to the general ministry. Most would now speak, as does *Baptism, Eucharist, and Ministry*, of "the calling of the whole people of God" to ministry. Within this community the Holy Spirit "bestows . . . diverse and complementary gifts [for] . . . service within the community and to the world."[73]

The ordained ministry is based on providential gifts or charisms recognized by ecclesiastical acknowledgment or ordination. The work of the ordained consists chiefly in assembling and building up "the body of Christ by proclaiming and teaching the Word of God, by celebrating the sacraments, and by guiding the life of the community in its worship, its mission and its caring ministry."[74] While acknowledging "a variety of forms which existed at different places and times" of ministry in the New Testament, *Baptism, Eucharist and Ministry* points out the eventual evolution of "a threefold pattern of bishop, presbyter and deacon" and urges churches lacking such a formal structure to consider its advantages.[75] Episcopacy is seen as one way of expressing the continuity of the historic faith.

Recent ordination rites have become increasingly similar. Many have drawn on the same sources from the third and fourth century. Methodists and Episcopalians have recovered a permanent diaconate although Lutherans recently rejected this. Most new rites now focus on the primary act of ordination by the laying on of hands in the context of prayer invoking the Holy Spirit for the necessary gifts and graces.

In the United Methodist rites, the bishop alone lays hands on deacons; the bishop, elders, and laypeople lay hands on elders; and bishops and representatives of other communions lay hands on bishops.[76] The Episcopal rite provides for the ordination of bishops, priests, and deacons by laying on of hands in a prayer of invocation.[77] Both Methodists and Episcopalians now place ordinations in the context of the eucharist, and the United Methodist rites have a special eucharistic prayer.

Lutherans speak of one order of ordained ministry. The focus is laying on of hands by other pastors in the context of prayer.[78] At present, Presbyterians are still in the process of liturgical revision of their ordination rites.

Much has been accomplished, but every church is still deep in discussion about the meaning of ordained ministry. All are agreed that it must be seen in the context of service to and with the general ministry of the baptized. Mutual recognition of various forms of ordained ministry is becoming more and more common. The charismatic churches continually bring to the forefront new forms of ministry, although usually not ordained. Movement is slow but continuous, and that is a sign of hope in what ordained ministry can be in the twenty-first century.

CHRISTIAN BURIAL

It may seem strange to call Christian burial a sacrament, but the tradition extends at least as far back as Dionysius the Areopagite (sixth century) and as far forward as the Third Lateran Council of 1179. The Middle Ages made funerals awesome depictions of doom for the wicked. Imagination ran wild with images of hell's mouth and the hymn *Dies Irae* ("Day of Wrath") shaped popular piety. In short, the church tried to scare people out of hell by scaring hell out of them! Death was largely about fear.

Various reformers reacted by trying to recover the early Christian image of hope in the face of death. They did not have to react to funerals as a sacrament but did have to reject many customs in their efforts to make the funeral of a Christian a sign of hope. Luther speaks of having "abolished the popish abominations, such as vigils, masses for the dead, processions, purgatory, and all other hocus-pocus on behalf of the dead."[79] Instead, he would institute "comforting hymns of the forgiveness of sins, of rest, sleep, life, and of the resurrection of departed Christians."

Any reference to purgatory was banished from Protestant worship, but this raised questions about prayer for the dead. Some denied any purpose in such prayer since it might be misinterpreted as implying the existence of purgatory and, even worse, the pope's control over the same. Cranmer's 1549 eucharistic prayer prays for these "departed hence from us." This disappeared in 1552, but in 1662 God is blessed for the departed and asked to give us grace to "follow their good examples." John Wesley kept the same language, but these words vanished in American Methodism.

The Reformed tradition reduced funeral ceremonies to the minimum. John Knox's service book of 1556, based on Calvin's, simply says, "The Corpse is reverently brought to the grave, accompanied with the congregation, without any further ceremonies, which being buried, the minister goes to the church, if it be not far off, and makes some comfortable exhortation to the people, touching on death, and resurrection."[80] The whole emphasis is didactic. The *Westminster Directory* says the body is brought "from the house to the place appointed for public burial, and there immediately interred, without any Ceremony." However, the minister may preach to "put them in remembrance of their duty."[81] John Wesley's service tries not to presume upon the ultimate destination of the soul of the deceased.[82]

Various factors led to the commercialization of death. Tombstones became common for ordinary people in the seventeenth century, coffins became usual in the eighteenth, and embalming in the nineteenth. Professional undertakers often took over funerals altogether, leaving churches in an ambiguous role.[83]

Recent decades have seen the churches reassert their role in the care of the dead. New rites stress two functions of the Christian funeral: comforting the bereaved and committing the deceased to God's care. Comforting involves acknowledging the reality of death and yet proclaiming the trustworthiness of God. Death becomes the supreme challenge to faith and most of the new rites consist chiefly of proclaiming the Christian faith through scripture, psalmody, hymnody, and prayer in the face of death. An effort is made to make funerals distinctively a service of Christian worship in the case of Christian deceased. More funerals are being held in churches, and some congregations have even gone so far as to install columbaria for the ashes of those cremated, making the church the sanctuary for their remains.

The new United Methodist rites are entitled "Services of Death and Resurrection."[84] They include an order for holy communion with its own eucharistic prayer. Provisions are also made for the burial of a child, an untimely or tragic death, and for a person who did not profess the Christian faith. Prayers are provided for ministry with the dying, following death, a wake, and for a stillborn child. All this is an extraordinary development from the resources previously available.

The Episcopal Church shows sensitivity in providing two services for "The Burial of the Dead," one in traditional language and one in contemporary.[85] One prayer asks that the deceased, "increasing in knowledge and love of thee, . . . may go from strength to strength in the life of perfect service in thy heavenly kingdom,"[86] an indication of prayer for the dead without toppling into purgatory.

The Lutheran "Burial of the Dead" seeks to emphasize the hope of the resurrection. It forbids social or fraternal societies from participating but stresses the use of a pall, procession to the grave, and casting of earth on the coffin.[87] It was left to the Presbyterians to do the most thorough job in providing resources for Christian burial. "The Funeral: A Service of Witness to the Resurrection"[88] begins with placing the pall and may open with a remembrance of baptism into the death and resurrection of Christ Jesus. Psalms, lessons, the Apostles' Creed, and prayers sound notes of thanksgiving and hope. Provision is made for the eucharist with a special eucharistic prayer. Committal possibilities are provided for earth burial, burial at sea, cremation, and ashes at a columbarium. All of this is a major advance over what was previously available. From mere burial rites we have moved to a process of care for the dead as well as for the bereaved. The churches owe much to this generation of liturgical revisers.

All the commonly called sacraments are in a process of evolution and have become important sources for pastoral care.

CHAPTER SEVEN

Future Prospects

Half a century ago, Paul Tillich wrote in *The Protestant Era* that "the solution of the problem of 'nature and sacrament' is today a task on which the very destiny of Protestantism depends."[1] He considered it necessary "if Protestantism is to come to its full realization" that a "rediscovery of the sacramental sphere" occur. This would involve the realization that "natural objects can become bearers of transcendent power and meaning . . . by being brought into the context of the history of salvation."[2]

If Tillich were alive today, he would probably be both dismayed at the slowness in achieving this in some parts of Protestantism and amazed at the speed with which it has moved in other parts. Stubborn resistance to sacramental realism was nothing new in Tillich's time or in ours. Frequently it occurs among the most theologically conservative, whose minds were made up by the Enlightenment. Yet many liberal theologians have the same problem with accepting supernatural use of the natural. On the other hand, Tillich would be astonished at how much has changed in the direction of a richer sacramental life in his native Lutheran tradition and among many other Protestant groups.

The major impediment to a richer sacramental life still seems to be the reluctance to see sacraments as present acts of God rather than merely human memories of God's acts in the past. It is difficult for many Protestants to conceive of sacraments as God's self-giving. Little sense of sacramental efficacy survives among many Protestants and, for that matter, among not a few Roman Catholics. For many, the Enlightenment decisively severed any connection between the spiritual and the physical.

A more recent threat has come about through much of the church growth movement, which tries to minimize the gap between church and culture. While this has been successful in many instances in reaching out to the unchurched or the previously churched, it has tended to further marginalize the sacraments, the church year, and the lectionary as intrinsically irrelevant or even in conflict with our culture. On the other hand, the fastest growing denomination in the U.S.A. is the Roman Catholic, which has no hesitation in presenting the sacraments as an intrinsic part of Christian faith. The Rite of Christian Initiation of Adults structures the whole conversion process around preparation for and reception of the sacraments of initiation.

A third obstacle to a richer sacramental life is often careless or unthinking practice. The practice of rebaptism undercuts any sense of the activity of God in the previous baptism. Sloppy or careless celebrations of the eucharist weaken and destroy faith in it as communion with God. The lack of teaching the meaning of the sacraments has left a generation sacramentally illiterate.

The positive signs, though, are impressive. As we have recounted already, most churches that use liturgical texts have the best available in history. That the new Protestant and Roman Catholic rites are remarkably similar is a sign of a common search for quality. Indeed, the chief difference between a United Methodist eucharist and a Roman Catholic one is that United Methodists use real bread and Roman Catholics use real wine.

Changes have been felt in other ways than verbal texts. Thousands of churches have been built or remodeled to make the font or pool and the altar-table central along with the pulpit. This means careful attention has been shown to their location and design so that they can function with theological integrity. Hundreds of new hymns have been written and old ones rescued from obscurity to allow the people to express the meaning of the sacraments. Compare the sections in old hymnals on baptism with the new.

141

In most Protestant churches, baptism has become a public act of the whole community, not just a private ceremony. And the eucharist is now celebrated weekly as the main Sunday service in thousands of Episcopal and Lutheran churches and some United Methodist and Presbyterian congregations. Thousands of the latter two have moved to monthly celebrations. Frequency often makes the eucharist more meaningful; meaningfulness demands more frequency.

THE CHALLENGE OF THE FUTURE

The chapters that have preceded this one have chronicled the rich diversity of Protestant practice and faith in the sacraments. The richness of Protestant sacramental worship consists in its diversity and its consequent ability to serve a wide variety of peoples at different times and places.

This will be all the more relevant in the future as Protestantism becomes even more of a worldwide presence. No longer can we think of Protestantism in purely European and North American terms. There are now more Anglicans in Uganda than in the U.S.A., more Presbyterians in Korea than in Scotland and the U.S.A. combined. This means that the ability to relate the sacraments to different peoples and cultures must not only continue but accelerate. We truly need to think in terms of "all people that on earth do dwell."

But this is also a two-way street or a multilayered intersection, because we can learn much from other regions of the world. In some ways, they may be more open to sacramental worship, not having been as conditioned by the Enlightenment to desacralize the physical world. Meaningful signs in these cultures may be useful for us: gestures, such as carrying vessels on one's head; furniture, such as foot-high tables; customs, such as tying a necklace at weddings; all may show us things our culture has neglected. We must not be defensive about fashions peculiar to Western culture when other cultures have so much to offer, especially as we continue to work out our own problems.

Several items are working their way to the front of the agendas of many churches at present. One of them is to restore the unity of Christian initiation to a single time and place, at whatever age, so that one is no longer halfway a part of the church. Several churches have made great strides in this direction although the changes have been frequently misunderstood.

Related is the recovery of the paschal nature of baptism so that the new Christian is seen as dying and rising in Christ. Easter baptisms are becoming more common, but it takes time to reverse the last thousand years of history.

The move to baptism by immersion is not needed by Baptists and Disciples of Christ, who have shown a stronger sacramental sense in stressing the sign values of cleansing and of dying and rising with Christ than the older churches. For the older traditions, reversing five or six hundred years of Western history and recovering baptism of infants by immersion or dipping is a very slow process. The first step would be more adequate baptismal fonts or pools. This process can be observed in some Roman Catholic parishes where the initiative has come on a local basis.

The recovery of children's communion is underway but again that means bucking eight hundreds years of Western malpractice. But both theology and developmental psychology encourage us to take seriously the consequences of baptism. One's being is at stake, not just one's thought processes.

Much progress has been made in seeking inclusive language but much remains to be done. The service books of the 1970s will eventually need to be redone. (The Lutherans, for instance, always make the devil masculine.) Only the United Methodist rite even mentions children ("And now, with the confidence of children of God, let us pray"). The service books of the 1990s will eventually need fine tuning, if not drastic revision. And all of them will eventually become dated as biblical, historical, and theological scholarship progresses.

It may be clear from what has been written in previous chapters that theological shifts are sometimes necessary. We can hope that the eschatological nature of baptism will become more apparent just as eschatology has reappeared in the new eucharistic rites. Regarding the eucharist, it is hoped that Protestants and Roman Catholics together may get beyond the Reformation impasse over eucharistic sacrifice. The biblical and early church imagery of sacrifice is too important to be abandoned altogether. Our changing concepts of the environment and the global human community will call us beyond Episcopal eucharistic prayer C. Above all, we must seek balanced and comprehensive statements of God's action as experienced in the sacraments

143

over the centuries. In these efforts, we can be partners with a global community of Protestant worshipers.

And finally, these things will have little meaning unless continuing effort is made to teach them. Calvin's second ministerial office was the teacher. We can have the best liturgical texts, the best arranged church buildings, and wonderful church music, but their impact will be blunted unless the sacraments as efficacious means of God's action in our lives are explained and proclaimed. We have made much progress in teaching Christian worship in American seminaries in the last forty years. But ministers must carry on the teaching so their congregations are gathered up in wonder at celebrating Christ's presence in our midst.

NOTES

1. Sacramentality

1. Steven Ozment, *The Age of Reform: 1250–1550: An Intellectual and Religious History of Late Medieval and Reformation Europe* (New Haven: Yale University Press, 1980), p. 211.
2. *The Letters of Stephen Gardiner*, ed. James A. Muller (New York: Macmillan, 1933). (Spelling modernized.)
3. *The Canons and Decrees of the Council of Trent*, trans. H. J. Schroeder (Rockford, Ill.: Tan Books, 1978), p. 151.
4. Peter Lombard, *The Four Books of Sentences*, Book 4, trans. Owen R. Orr, in *A Scholastic Miscellany: Anselm to Ockham*, ed. and trans. Eugene R. Fairweather, Library of Christian Classics 10 (Philadelphia: Westminster Press, 1956), p. 344.
5. Norman Paul Tanner, *Decrees of the Ecumenical Councils: From Nicea I to Vatican II*, vol. 1 (Washington, D.C.: Georgetown University Press, 1990), p. 315.
6. Thomas Aquinas, *Summa Theologica*, Part III, Question 64, Second Article, trans. Fathers of the English Dominican Province, vol. 2 (New York: Benziger Brothers, 1947), p. 2367.
7. Thomas Aquinas sums up medieval sacramental doctrine in "De Articulis fidei et ecclesiae sacramentis," in *Opuscula theologica*, vol. 1 (Turin: Marietti, 1954), pp. 147-51. This treatise was followed closely, with some abbreviations, in what became dogma in the papal bull *Exsultate Deo* of 22 November 1439, the "Decree for the Armenians." For translation, see James F. White, *Documents of Christian Worship: Descriptive and Interpretive Sources* (Louisville: Westminster/John Knox Press, 1992).
8. Thomas Aquinas, *Summa Theologica*, Suppl. XXX, Question 30, First Article, vol. 3 (New York: Benziger Brothers, 1948), p. 2672.
9. *A Treatise on the New Testament, That Is, the Holy Mass*, trans. Jeremiah J. Schindel and E. Theodore Bachmann, in *Luther's Works*, vol. 35 (Philadelphia: Muhlenberg Press, 1960), pp. 79-111.
10. *The Babylonian Captivity of the Church*, trans. A. T. W. Steinhäuser, Frederick C. Ahrens, and Abdel Ross Wentz, in *Luther's Works*, vol. 36 (Philadelphia: Muhlenberg Press, 1959), p. 124.
11. Ibid.

12. Ibid. , p. 57.
13. Ibid., p. 58.
14. Ibid., p. 67.
15. The Small Catechism, in *The Book of Concord*, trans. Theodore G. Tappert (Philadelphia: Fortress Press, 1959), p. 349.
16. The Large Catechism, in *Book of Concord*, p. 439.
17. Ibid., p. 454.
18. The Augsburg Confession, Latin text, in *Book of Concord*, p. 35.
19. Ulrich Zwingli, *Commentary on True and False Religion*, ed. Samuel Macauley Jackson and Clarence Nevin Heller (1929; reprint, Durham, N.C.: Labyrinth Press, 1981), p. 181.
20. Ibid., p. 184.
21. Ulrich Zwingli, *An Exposition of the Faith*, in *Zwingli and Bullinger*, ed. and trans. G. W. Bromiley, Library of Christian Classics 24 (Philadelphia: Westminster Press, 1953), p. 263.
22. Ibid., pp. 262-65.
23. John Calvin, *Institutes of the Christian Religion*, ed. John T. McNeill, trans. Ford Lewis Battles, Library of Christian Classics 20-21 (Philadelphia: Westminster Press, 1960), p. 1277.
24. Ibid., p. 1278.
25. Ibid.
26. Ibid., p. 1284.
27. Ibid., p. 1293.
28. Ibid., p. 1291. Compare this with E. Schillebeeckx' assertion that Christ is the primordial sacrament, *Christ the Sacrament of the Encounter with God*, trans. Paul Barrett, Mark Schoof, and Laurence Bright (New York: Sheed and Ward, 1963), p. 15.
29. Calvin, *Institutes*, p. 1292.
30. Articles of Religion, in *The Book of Common Prayer* (New York: Church Hymnal Corporation, 1979), p. 872.
31. Ibid., p. 873.
32. Scotch Confession of Faith, in Philip Schaff, *The Creeds of Christendom* (1877; reprint, Grand Rapids: Baker Book House, 1969), vol. 3, pp. 467-68. (Spelling modernized.)
33. Robert Barclay, *An Apology for the True Christian Divinity* (Manchester: William Irwin, 1869), p. 215.
34. Ibid., p. 240.
35. The Westminster Confession of Faith, in Schaff, *Creeds of Christendom*, vol. 3, pp. 660-61.
36. Immanuel Kant, *Religion Within the Limits of Reason Alone*, trans. Theodore M. Green and Hoyt H. Hudson (New York: Harper & Row, 1960), p. 188.
37. Lester Ruth, "A Little Heaven Below: Quarterly Meetings as Seasons of Grace in Early American Methodism" (unpublished Ph.D. dissertation, University of Notre Dame, 1996).
38. "Future of Faith Worries Catholic Leaders," *New York Times*, June 1, 1994, p. 88.
39. *Babylonian Captivity*, in *Luther's Works*, vol. 36, p. 86.
40. Ibid., p. 91.
41. Ibid., p. 92.
42. Ibid., p. 107.
43. Ibid., p. 118.
44. Ibid., p. 124.
45. Large Catechism, in *Book of Concord*, p. 436.
46. Beverley Nitschke, "The Third Sacrament? Confession and Forgiveness in the *Lutheran Book of Worship*" (unpublished Ph.D. dissertation, University of Notre Dame, 1988).
47. Augsburg Confession, in *Book of Concord*, Latin text, p. 61.
48. Caspar Schwenckfeld, "An Answer to Luther's Malediction," in *Spiritual and Anabaptist Writers*, ed. George H. Williams, Library of Christian Classics 25 (Philadelphia: Westminster Press, 1957), p. 168.
49. Calvin, *Institutes*, p. 1296.
50. Ibid., p. 1476.
51. Ibid., p. 1450.
52. Ibid., p. 1463.

53. Ibid., p. 1466.
54. Ibid., p. 1468.
55. Articles of Religion, in *Book of Common Prayer*, pp. 872.
56. *A Directory for the Publique Worship of God* (Bramcote, Notts.: Grove Books, 1980), p. 24.
57. James F. White, *Sacraments as God's Self Giving* (Nashville: Abingdon Press, 1983), pp. 70-92.
58. F. D. Maurice, *The Kingdom of Christ* (London: James Clarke & Co., 1959).
59. Nan Dearmer, *The Life of Percy Dearmer* (London: Jonathan Cape, 1940).
60. A. G. Hebert, *Liturgy and Society: The Function of the Church in the Modern World* (London: Faber and Faber, 1935).
61. James F. White, *The Worldliness of Worship* (New York: Oxford University Press, 1967), p. 93.
62. John Macquarrie, *A Guide to the Sacraments* (New York: Continuum, 1997), p. 8.

2. Baptism in Practice and Controversy

1. *The Babylonian Captivity of the Church*, trans. A. T. W. Steinhäuser, Frederick C. Ahrens, and Abdel Ross Wentz, in *Luther's Works*, vol. 36 (Philadelphia: Muhlenberg Press, 1959), p. 57.
2. Hughes Oliphant Old, *The Shaping of the Reformed Baptismal Rite in the Sixteenth Century* (Grand Rapids: Eerdmans, 1992), p. 265.
3. *Babylonian Captivity*, in *Luther's Works*, vol. 36, p. 68.
4. "Order of Baptism," and "Order of Baptism Newly Revised," both trans. Paul Zeller Strodach and Ulrich S. Leupold, in *Luther's Works*, vol. 53 (Philadelphia: Fortress Press, 1965), pp. 100 and 109.
5. *The Holy and Blessed Sacrament of Baptism*, trans. Charles M. Jacobs and E. Theodore Bachmann, in *Luther's Works*, vol. 35 (Philadelphia: Muhlenberg Press, 1960), p. 29.
6. Old, *Shaping of the Reformed Baptismal Rite*, p. 278.
7. J. D. C. Fisher, *Christian Initiation: Baptism in the Medieval West* (London: S.P.C.K., 1965), p. 136.
8. The Canons and Decrees of the Council of Trent, trans. J. Waterworth, in Philip Schaff, *The Creeds of Christendom* (1877; reprint, Grand Rapids: Baker Book House, 1969), vol. 2, p. 174.
9. John Calvin, *Institutes of the Christian Religion*, ed. John T. McNeill, trans. Ford Lewis Battles, Library of Christian Classics 20-21 (Philadelphia: Westminster Press, 1960), pp. 1321-23.
10. *Tertullian's Homily on Baptism*, trans. Ernest Evans (London: S.P.C.K., 1964), p. 39.
11. *Blessed Sacrament of Baptism*, in *Luther's Works*, vol. 35, p. 34.
12. Ibid., p. 36.
13. Ibid., p. 42.
14. *Babylonian Captivity*, in *Luther's Works*, vol. 36, p. 59.
15. The Large Catechism, in *The Book of Concord*, trans. Theodore G. Tappert (Philadelphia: Fortress Press, 1959), p. 442.
16. Ibid., p. 445.
17. *Babylonian Captivity*, in *Luther's Works*, vol. 36, p. 73.
18. Large Catechism, in *Book of Concord*, p. 444.
19. "Order of Baptism," in *Luther's Works*, vol. 53, p. 97.
20. George H. Williams, *The Radical Reformation* (Philadelphia: Westminster Press, 1962), p. 120.
21. Rollin Stely Armour, *Anabaptist Baptism: A Representative Study* (Scottdale, Pa.: Herald Press, 1966), p. 19.
22. "A Form for Water Baptism," in *Balthasar Hubmaier: Theologian of Anabaptism*, trans. H. Wayne Pipkin and John H. Yoder (Scottdale, Pa.: Herald Press, 1989), p. 389.
23. "On the Christian Ban," in *Balthasar Hubmaier*, p. 417.
24. *Foundations of Christian Doctrine*, in *The Complete Writings of Menno Simons*, ed. John C. Wenger, trans. Leonard Verduin (Scottdale, Pa.: Herald Press, 1956), p. 120.
25. *Of Baptism*, in *Zwingli and Bullinger*, ed. and trans. G. W. Bromiley, Library of Christian Classics 24 (Philadelphia: Westminster Press, 1953), p. 146.
26. Armour, *Anabaptist Baptism*, p. 141.

27. G. R. Beasley-Murray, *Baptism in the New Testament* (Exeter: Paternoster Press, 1972), p. 125.
28. James F. White, *Protestant Worship: Traditions in Transition* (Louisville: Westminster/John Knox Press, 1989), pp. 171-91.
29. Charles R. Hohenstein, "The Revisions of the Rites of Baptism in the Methodist Episcopal Church, 1784–1939" (unpublished Ph.D. dissertation, University of Notre Dame, 1990), pp. 89-127.
30. Horace Bushnell, *Christian Nurture* (1847; reprint, New Haven: Yale University Press, 1967), p. 4.
31. Karl Barth, *The Teaching of the Church Regarding Baptism*, trans. Ernest A. Payne (London: SCM Press, 1948), p. 9.
32. Ibid., p. 27.
33. Oscar Cullmann, *Baptism in the New Testament*, trans. J. K. S. Reid, Studies in Biblical Theology 1 (London: S.P.C.K. Press, 1950).
34. Joachim Jeremias, *Infant Baptism in the First Four Centuries*, trans. David Cairns (Philadelphia: Westminster Press, 1962) and *The Origins of Infant Baptism*, trans. Dorothea M. Barton (Naperville, Ill.: Allenson, 1963); Kurt Aland, *Did the Early Church Baptize Infants?* trans. G. R. Beasley-Murray (Philadelphia: Westminster Press, 1963).
35. Aidan Kavanagh, *The Shape of Baptism: The Rite of Christian Initiation* (New York: Pueblo Press, 1978), p. 110.
36. *Instruction on Infant Baptism* (Vatican City: Vatican Polyglot Press, 1980), p. 16.
37. *Baptism, Eucharist and Ministry* (Geneva: World Council of Churches, 1982), p. 6.
38. "Order of Baptism," in *Luther's Works*, vol. 53, p. 97. Italics mine.
39. *Blessed Sacrament of Baptism*, in *Luther's Works*, vol. 35, p. 29.
40. *Babylonian Captivity*, in *Luther's Works*, vol. 36, p. 68.
41. See Old, *Shaping of the Reformed Baptismal Rite*, p. 265.
42. Calvin, *Institutes*, p. 1320.
43. *The First and Second Prayer Books of Edward VI* (London: Everyman's Library, 1964), p. 240. (Spelling modernized.)
44. Charles Wheatly, *A Rational Illustration of the Book of Common Prayer* (3rd ed., 1720; reprint, London: Henry G. Bohn, 1852), p. 350.
45. *John Wesley's Prayer Book* (Akron: OSL Publications, 1991), pp. 142 and 148.
46. *First and Second Prayer Books*, pp. 237, 241, 398.
47. "The Millenary Petition," in *Documents Illustrative of English Church History*, ed. Henry Gee and William John Hardy (London: Macmillan, 1910), p. 509.
48. *A Directory for the Publique Worship of God* (Bramcote, Notts.: Grove Books, 1980), p. 20.
49. Illustrated in James F. White, *Documents of Christian Worship: Descriptive and Interpretive Sources* (Louisville: Westminster/John Knox Press, 1992), p. 45.
50. Johan van Parys, "A Place for Baptism: New Trends in Baptismal Architecture Since the Second Vatican Council," (unpublished Ph.D. dissertation, University of Notre Dame, 1998).
51. A. A. Parker, *The People's Hand-Book on Immersion, Infant Baptism, Close Communion, and Plan of Salvation: or Justification by Water Versus Justification by Faith with a Chapter on the Campbellite* (Nashville: Publishing House of the M.E. Church, South, 1893), p. 6.
52. "Draft Ecclesiastical Ordinances, September & October 1541," in *Calvin: Theological Treatises*, trans. J. K. S. Reid, Library of Christian Classics 22 (Philadelphia: Westminster Press, 1954), p. 66.
53. The Augsburg Confession, Latin text, in *Book of Concord*, p. 33.
54. Calvin, *Institutes*, p. 1321.
55. Ibid., p. 1323.
56. Ibid.
57. Calvin, "La Forme d'administrer le baptesme," in *Ioannis Calvini Opera Quae Supersunt Omnia* (Brunswick: C. A. Schwetschke and Sons, 1867), vol. 6, pp. 183-91.
58. For example, see *American Church Silver of the Seventeenth and Eighteenth Centuries* (Boston: Museum of Fine Arts, 1911).
59. *First and Second Prayer Books*, pp. 236 and 394.
60. Stephen P. Dorsey, *Early English Churches in America, 1607–1807* (New York: Oxford University Press, 1952), p. 19.

61. *Babylonian Captivity*, in *Luther's Works*, vol. 36, p. 91.
62. Martin Luther, quoted in J. D. C. Fisher, *Christian Initiation: The Reformation Period* (London: S.P.C.K., 1970), p. 173.
63. Ibid., p. 202.
64. Calvin, *Institutes*, p. 1461.
65. Ibid., p. 1452.
66. *First and Second Prayer Books*, p. 251.
67. *The Doctrines and Discipline of the Methodist Episcopal Church, 1864* (Cincinnati: Poe & Hitchcock, 1866), pp. 145-49.
68. Ruth Meyers, *Continuing the Reformation: Re-Visioning Baptism in the Episcopal Church* (New York: Church Publishing, 1997). Cf. also the United Methodist *Christian Initiation Series*, 5 vols. (Nashville: Discipleship Resources, 1996–1998).

3. Baptismal Meanings

1. George H. Williams, *The Radical Reformation* (Philadelphia: Westminster Press, 1962), p. 857.
2. *Baptism, Eucharist and Ministry* (Geneva: World Council of Churches, 1982), p. 3.
3. *The United Methodist Book of Worship* (Nashville: The United Methodist Publishing House, 1992), p. 90.
4. *Lutheran Book of Worship* (Minneapolis: Augsburg Publishing House, 1978), p. 121.
5. *Book of Common Worship* (Louisville: Westminster/John Knox Press, 1993), p. 412.
6. J. D. C. Fisher, *Christian Initiation: Baptism in the Medieval West* (London: S.P.C.K., 1965), p. 112.
7. *The Holy and Blessed Sacrament of Baptism*, trans. Charles M. Jacobs and E. Theodore Bachmann, in *Luther's Works*, vol. 35 (Philadelphia: Muhlenberg Press, 1960), p. 29.
8. Ibid., pp. 35-36.
9. *The Babylonian Captivity of the Church*, trans. A. T. W. Steinhäuser, Frederick C. Ahrens, and Abdel Ross Wentz, in *Luther's Works*, vol. 36 (Philadelphia: Muhlenberg Press, 1959), p. 124.
10. The Augsburg Confession, Latin text, in *The Book of Concord*, trans. Theodore G. Tappert (Philadelphia: Fortress Press, 1959), p. 33.
11. The Schleitheim Confession, in *Legacy of Michael Sattler*, ed. and trans. John Howard Yoder (Scottdale, Pa.: Herald Press, 1973), p. 36.
12. Conrad Grebel, "Letter to Thomas Müntzer," in *Spiritual and Anabaptist Writers*, ed. George H. Williams, Library of Christian Classics 25 (Philadelphia: Westminster Press, 1957), pp. 80-81.
13. A Christian Catechism, in *Balthasar Hubmaier: Theologian of Anabaptism*, trans. H. Wayne Pipkin and John H. Yoder, (Scottdale, Pa.: Herald Press, 1989), p. 349.
14. "On Fraternal Admonition," in *Balthasar Hubmaier*, p. 380.
15. *Of Baptism*, in *Zwingli and Bullinger*, ed. and trans. G. W. Bromiley, Library of Christian Classics 24 (Philadelphia: Westminster Press, 1953), p. 156.
16. John Calvin, *Institutes of the Christian Religion*, ed. John T. McNeill, trans. Ford Lewis Battles, Library of Christian Classics 20-21 (Philadelphia: Westminster Press, 1960), p. 1304.
17. Ibid., p. 1305.
18. Ibid., p. 1344.
19. *The Book of Common Prayer* (New York: Church Hymnal Corporation, 1979), p. 873.
20. The Westminster Confession of Faith, in Philip Schaff, *Creeds of Christendom* (1877; reprint, Grand Rapids: Baker Book House, 1969), vol. 3, p. 662.
21. *Baptism, Eucharist and Ministry*, p. 2.
22. *United Methodist Book of Worship*, p. 90.
23. *Lutheran Book of Worship*, p. 122.
24. *Book of Common Prayer*, p. 307.
25. *Book of Common Worship*, pp. 411, 404.
26. *Egeria's Travels*, trans. John Wilkinson (London: S.P.C.K., 1971), pp. 143-46.
27. *Blessed Sacrament of Baptism*, in *Luther's Works*, vol. 35, p. 30.
28. *Babylonian Captivity*, in *Luther's Works*, vol. 36, p. 67.

29. Ibid., p. 68.
30. *To the Christian Nobility of the German Nation Concerning the Reform of the Christian Estate*, trans. Charles M. Jacobs and James Atkinson, in *Luther's Works*, vol. 44 (Philadelphia: Fortress Press, 1966), p. 129.
31. *Of Baptism*, in *Zwingli and Bullinger*, p. 151.
32. Schleitheim Confession, in *Legacy*, p. 36.
33. Hans Hut, in *Anabaptism in Outline*, ed. Walter Klaassen (Scottdale, Pa.: Herald Press, 1981), pp. 169-70.
34. Dirk Philips, "Christian Baptism," in *Anabaptism in Outline*, pp. 184-85.
35. Calvin, *Institutes*, p. 1307.
36. Westminster Confession, in Schaff, *Creeds of Christendom*, vol. 3, p. 662.
37. *A Directory for the Publique Worship of God* (Bramcote, Notts.: Grove Books, 1980), p. 20.
38. Comment by Professor Arlo Duba.
39. *United Methodist Book of Worship*, p. 90.
40. *Book of Common Prayer*, p. 306.
41. *Lutheran Book of Worship*, p. 122.
42. *Book of Common Worship*, p. 410.
43. *Babylonian Captivity*, in *Luther's Works*, vol. 36, p. 73.
44. The Large Catechism, in *Book of Concord*, p. 436.
45. *Of Baptism*, in *Zwingli and Bullinger*, p. 146.
46. "A Form for Water Baptism," in *Balthasar Hubmaier*, p. 389.
47. Hans Denck, "Recantation," in *Anabaptism in Outline*, p. 168.
48. Pilgrim Marpeck, "Admonition," in *Anabaptism in Outline*, p. 182.
49. Catechism of the Church of Geneva, in *Calvin: Theological Treatises* trans. J. K. S. Reid, Library of Christian Classics 22 (Philadelphia: Westminster Press, 1954), p. 133.
50. Calvin, *Institutes*, p. 1313.
51. Ibid., p. 1323.
52. Ibid., p. 1016.
53. Ibid., p. 1023.
54. Ibid., p. 1341.
55. Articles of Religion, in *Book of Common Prayer*, p. 873.
56. Westminster Confession, in Schaff, *Creeds of Christendom*, vol. 3, p. 662.
57. *A Directory for Publique Worship*, p. 21.
58. *Doctrines and Discipline of the Methodist Episcopal Church, 1864* (Cincinnati: Poe & Hitchcock, 1866), pp. 145-49.
59. *United Methodist Book of Worship*, p. 93.
60. *Baptism, Eucharist and Ministry*, p. 3.
61. *United Methodist Book of Worship*, p. 87.
62. Ibid., p. 94.
63. *Book of Common Prayer*, pp. 306-7.
64. *Lutheran Book of Worship*, p. 121.
65. Ibid., p. 125.
66. *Book of Common Worship*, p. 405.
67. Ibid., p. 414.
68. Ibid., pp. 406-7.
69. Zwingli, *Commentary On True and False Religion*, ed. Samuel Macauley Jackson and Clarence Nevin Heller (1929; reprint, Durham, N.C.: Labyrinth Press, 1981), p. 187.
70. *Of Baptism*, in *Zwingli and Bullinger*, pp. 137-38.
71. A Christian Catechism, in *Balthasar Hubmaier*, p. 349.
72. Hans Hut, in *Anabaptism in Outline*, p. 169.
73. Calvin, *Institutes*, p. 1344.
74. Ibid., p. 1457.
75. *The First and Second Prayer Books of Edward VI* (London: Everyman's Library, 1964), pp. 236, 394; 241; 245.
76. Robert Barclay, *Apology for the True Christian Divinity* (Manchester: William Irwin, 1869), p. 257.

77. Gregory Dix, *The Theology of Confirmation in Relation to Baptism* (London: Dacre, 1946).
78. See, for instance, G. W. H. Lampe, *The Seal of the Spirit* (London: S.P.C.K., 1967).
79. *Baptism, Eucharist and Ministry*, p. 2.
80. *United Methodist Book of Worship*, pp. 90-91.
81. *Book of Common Prayer*, pp. 307-8.
82. *Lutheran Book of Worship*, p. 122.
83. *Book of Common Worship*, p. 411.
84. Ibid., p. 413.
85. Ibid., p. 414.
86. Peter Riedeman, *Account of Our Religion, Doctrine, and Faith*, in *Anabaptism in Outline*, p. 182.
87. Calvin, *Institutes*, p. 1325.
88. Ibid., p. 1340.
89. Ibid., p. 1348.
90. *First and Second Prayer Books*, pp. 236-37, 239, 241.
91. J. C. S. Nias, *Gorham and the Bishop of Exeter* (London: S.P.C.K., 1951).
92. *United Methodist Book of Worship*, pp. 87, 90-91.
93. *Book of Common Prayer*, pp. 306-7.
94. *Lutheran Book of Worship*, p. 121.
95. *Book of Common Worship*, p. 412.
96. Cf. James F. White, *Sacraments as God's Self Giving* (Nashville: Abingdon, 1983), pp. 93-113.
97. *Tertullian's Homily on Baptism*, trans. Ernest Evans (London: S.P.C.K., 1964), p. 39.
98. *Lutheran Book of Worship*, p. 124.
99. *United Methodist Book of Worship*, p. 88.
100. *Book of Common Prayer*, p. 302.
101. *Book of Common Worship*, p. 407.

4. The Eucharist in Practice and Controversy

1. Edouard Dumoutet, *Le désir de voir l'hostie* (Paris: Beauchesne, 1926), p. 50.
2. *The Letters of Stephen Gardiner*, ed. James A. Muller (New York: Macmillan, 1933), p. 355.
3. Thomas Aquinas, *Summa Theologica*, Question 75, Article 4, trans. the Fathers of the English Dominican Province, vol. 3 (New York: Benziger Brothers, 1948), p. 2450.
4. Anselm of Canterbury, "Why God Became Man," in *A Scholastic Miscellany: Anselm to Ockham*, ed. and trans. Eugene R. Fairweather, Library of Christian Classics 10 (Philadelphia: Westminster Press, 1956), pp. 181-82.
5. Eamon Duffy, *The Stripping of the Altars: Traditional Religion in England, 1400–1580* (New Haven: Yale University Press, 1992), p. 302.
6. Ibid., p. 301.
7. Ibid., p. 354.
8. *Blessed Sacrament of the Holy and True Body of Christ, and the Brotherhoods*, trans. Jeremiah J. Schindel and E. Theodore Bachmann, in *Luther's Works*, vol. 35 (Philadelphia: Muhlenberg Press, 1960), p. 63.
9. *The Babylonian Captivity of the Church*, trans. A. T. W. Steinhäuser, Frederick C. Ahrens, and Abdel Ross Wentz, in *Luther's Works*, vol. 36 (Philadelphia: Muhlenberg Press, 1959), pp. 31-2.
10. Ibid., p. 35.
11. The Augsburg Confession, German text, in *Book of Concord*, trans. Theodore G. Tappert (Philadelphia: Fortress Press, 1959), p. 34.
12. *The Sacrament of the Body and Blood of Christ—Against the Fanatics*, trans. Frederick C. Ahrens, in *Luther's Works*, vol. 36, p. 342.
13. *Confession Concerning Christ's Supper*, trans. Robert H. Fischer, in *Luther's Works*, vol. 37 (Philadelphia: Muhlenberg Press, 1961), p. 212.
14. Ulrich Zwingli, *Commentary on True and False Religion*, ed. Samuel Macauley Jackson and Clarence Nevin Heller (1929; reprint, Durham, N.C.: Labyrinth Press, 1981), p. 227.
15. *An Exposition of the Faith*, in *Zwingli and Bullinger*, ed. and trans. G. W. Bromiley, Library of Christian Classics 24 (Philadelphia: Westminster Press, 1953), p. 248.

151

16. Ibid., p. 259.
17. "The Marburg Colloquy and the Marburg Articles," trans. Martin E. Lehmann, in *Luther's Works*, vol. 38 (Philadelphia: Fortress Press, 1971), pp. 70-71.
18. Ibid., p. 88.
19. *Foundation of Christian Doctrine*, in *The Complete Writings of Menno Simons*, ed. John C. Wenger, trans. Leonard Verduin (Scottdale, Pa.: Herald Press, 1956), p. 145. See also John D. Rempel, *The Lord's Supper in Anabaptism: A Study in the Christology of Balthasar Hubmaier, Pilgram Marpeck, and Dirk Philips* (Scottdale, Pa.: Herald Press, 1993).
20. John Calvin, *Institutes of the Christian Religion*, ed. John T. McNeill, trans. Ford Lewis Battles, Library of Christian Classics 20-21 (Philadelphia: Westminster Press, 1960), pp. 1393-94.
21. Ibid., p. 1401.
22. Ibid., p. 1364.
23. Ibid., p. 1371.
24. *Short Treatise on the Holy Supper of Our Lord and Only Saviour Jesus Christ*, in *Calvin: Theological Treatises*, trans. J. K. S. Reid, Library of Christian Classics 22 (Philadelphia: Westminster Press, 1954), p. 148.
25. Catechism of the Church of Geneva, in *Calvin: Theological Treatises*, p. 137.
26. Ibid.
27. Calvin, *Institutes*, p. 1405.
28. Ibid., p. 1403.
29. Ibid., p. 1382.
30. Brian Gerrish, *Grace and Gratitude: The Eucharistic Theology of John Calvin* (Minneapolis: Fortress Press, 1993), p. 167.
31. Diarmaid MacCulloch, *Thomas Cranmer: A Life* (New Haven: Yale University Press, 1996), pp. 614-15.
32. *The First and Second Prayer Books of Edward VI* (London: Everyman's Library, 1964), pp. 223, 225, 389.
33. The Scotch Confession of Faith, in Philip Schaff, *Creeds of Christendom* (1877; reprint, Grand Rapids: Baker Book House, 1969), vol. 3, pp. 468-69.
34. *A Directory for the Publique Worship of God* (Bramcote, Notts.: Grove Press, 1980), p. 22.
35. Benjamin Hoadly, *A Plain Account of the Nature and End of the Sacrament of the Lord's-Supper* (London: James, John, and Paul Knapton, 1735), p. 24.
36. *The Eucharistic Hymns of John and Charles Wesley*, ed. J. Ernest Rattenbury (London: Epworth Press, 1948), hymn 116, p. 232.
37. Ibid., hymn 72, p. 217.
38. Ibid., hymn 57, p. 213.
39. Lester Ruth, "A Little Heaven Below: Quarterly Meetings as Seasons of Grace in Early American Methodism" (unpublished Ph.D dissertation, University of Notre Dame, 1996).
40. John Nevin, *The Mystical Presence and Other Writings on the Eucharist*, ed. Bard Thompson and George H. Bricker (Philadelphia: United Church Press, 1966), p. 95.
41. James F. White, *The Cambridge Movement* (Cambridge: Cambridge University Press, 1962).
42. *The Methodist Hymnal* (Nashville: Methodist Publishing House, 1939), p. 530.
43. *The Methodist Hymnal* (Nashville: The Methodist Publishing House, 1966), 830.
44. *The United Methodist Book of Worship* (Nashville: The United Methodist Publishing House, 1992), p. 38.
45. *First and Second Prayer Books*, pp. 222, 389.
46. *The Book of Common Prayer* (New York: Church Hymnal Corporation, 1979), p. 363.
47. *Lutheran Book of Worship* (Minneapolis: Augsburg Publishing House, 1978), p. 90.
48. *Book of Common Worship* (Louisville: Westminster/John Knox Press, 1993), pp. 72, 132, 148.
49. The Canons and Decrees of the Council of Trent, trans. J. Waterworth, in Schaff, *Creeds of Christendom*, vol. 2, p. 138.
50. *Concerning the Order of Public Worship*, trans. Paul Zeller Strodach and Ulrich S. Leupold, in *Luther's Works*, vol. 53 (Philadelphia: Fortress Press, 1965), p. 11.
51. Ibid., p. 13.
52. Gunther Stiller, *Johann Sebastian Bach and Liturgical Life in Leipzig*, ed. Robin A. Leaver, trans. Herbert J. Bouman et al. (St. Louis: Concordia Press, 1984), p. 49.

53. Yngve Brilioth, *Eucharistic Faith and Practice: Evangelical and Catholic*, trans. A. G. Hebert (London: S.P.C.K., 1953), pp. 271-72.
54. Ulrich Zwingli, *Action or Use of the Lord's Supper*, in *Liturgies of the Western Church*, ed. Bard Thompson (1961; reprint, Minneapolis: Fortress Press, 1980), p. 151.
55. Calvin, *Institutes*, p. 1422.
56. Ibid., p. 1421.
57. "Draft Ecclesiastical Ordinances," in *Calvin: Theological Treatises*, p. 66.
58. *First and Second Prayer Books*, pp. 216, 382.
59. Ibid., p. 392.
60. Ibid.
61. *A Directory for Publique Worship*, p. 21.
62. Leigh Schmidt, *Holy Fairs: Scottish Communions and American Revivals in the Early Modern Period* (Princeton: Princeton University Press, 1989), p. 186.
63. *John Wesley*, ed. Albert C. Outler, (New York: Oxford University Press, 1964), pp. 332-44.
64. John Bowmer, *The Sacrament of The Lord's Supper in Early Methodism* (London: Epworth Press, 1951), p. 55.
65. *John Wesley's Prayer Book* (Akron: OSL Publications, 1991), p. ii.
66. Thomas Schattauer, "Announcement, Confession, and Lord's Supper in the Pastoral-Liturgical Work of Wilhelm Loehe" (unpublished Ph.D. dissertation, University of Notre Dame, 1990).
67. Donald Gray, *Earth and Altar: The Evolution of the Parish Communion in the Church of England to 1945* (London: Alcuin Club, 1968), pp. 153-215.
68. *To the Christian Nobility of the German Nation Concerning the Reform of the Christian Estate*, trans. Charles M. Jacobs and James Atkinson, in *Luther's Works*, vol. 44 (Philadelphia: Fortress Press, 1966), pp. 128-29.
69. Ralph F. Smith, *Luther, Ministry, and Ordination Rites in the Early Reformation Church* (New York: Peter Lang, 1995).
70. *John Wesley's Prayer Book*, p. ii.
71. Alexander Campbell, *The Christian System*, 2nd ed., (1866; reprint, New York: Arno Press, 1969), p. 311.
72. *The Private Mass and the Consecration of Priests*, trans. Martin E. Lehmann, in *Luther's Works*, vol. 38, p. 194.
73. "An Order of Mass and Communion for the Church at Wittenberg," trans. Paul Zeller Strodach and Ulrich S. Leupold; "The German Mass and Order of Service," trans. Augustus Steimle and Ulrich S. Leupold, in *Luther's Works*, vol. 53, pp. 19-40; 61-90. See also Irmgard Pahl, *Coena Domini I* (Freiburg: University Press, 1983), pp. 25-28.
74. See Hymns, trans. George MacDonald and Ulrich S. Leupold, in *Luther's Works*, vol. 53, pp. 189-309.
75. Margaret R. Miles, *Image as Insight: Visual Understanding in Western Christianity and Secular Culture* (Boston: Beacon Press, 1985), pp. 95-125.
76. Canons of the Council of Trent, in Schaff, *Creeds of Christendom*, vol. 2, p. 174.
77. *First and Second Prayer Books*, pp. 251, 409.
78. *A Directory for Publique Worship*, p. 21.
79. Calvin, *Institutes*, p. 1417.
80. Urban T. Holmes, *Young Children and the Eucharist* (New York: Seabury Press, 1982).
81. David R. Holeton, "Children and the Eucharist in the Tradition of the Church," in *Children at the Table: A Collection of Essays on Children and the Eucharist*, ed. Ruth A. Meyers (New York: Church Hymnal Corporation, 1995), pp. 11-18.
82. Kenneth W. Stevenson, "A Theological Reflection on the Experience of Inclusion/Exclusion at the Eucharist," in *Children at the Table*, pp. 42-56.
83. See *Human Disability and the Service of God: Reassessing Religious Practice*, ed. Nancy L. Eiesland and Don E. Saliers (Nashville: Abingdon Press, 1998) and Nancy L. Eiesland, *The Disabled God: Toward a Liberatory Theology of Disability* (Nashville: Abingdon Press, 1998).
84. *Babylonian Captivity*, in *Luther's Works*, vol. 36, p. 27.
85. Canons of the Council of Trent, in Schaff, *Creeds of Christendom*, vol. 2, p. 171.
86. Zwingli, *Action of the Lord's Supper*, in *Liturgies of the Western Church*, p. 151.

87. *First and Second Prayer Books*, pp. 230, 392.
88. Ibid., pp. 225, 389.
89. Ibid., p. 219.
90. Unpublished manuscript by Daniel Sack.
91. Gregory Dix, *The Shape of the Liturgy* (Westminster: Dacre Press, 1945), p. 103.

5. Eucharistic Meanings

1. Yngve Brilioth, *Eucharistic Faith and Practice, Evangelical and Catholic*, trans. A. G. Hebert (London: S.P.C.K., 1953).
2. Joseph Jungmann, *The Mass of the Roman Rite: Its Origins and Development*, 2 vols., trans. Francis A. Brunner (New York: Benziger Brothers, 1951, 1955).
3. Gregory Dix, *The Shape of the Liturgy* (Westminster: Dacre Press, 1945).
4. See Geoffrey Wainwright, *Eucharist and Eschatology* (London: Epworth Press, 1971) for a classic statement.
5. J. Ernest Rattenbury, *The Eucharistic Hymns of John and Charles Wesley* (London: Epworth Press, 1948), hymn 93, p. 225.
6. Ibid., hymn 100, p. 227; hymn 112, p. 230.
7. *The Liturgy and Other Divine Offices of the Church* (London: H. J. Glaisher, 1922), p. 17.
8. Dix, *Shape of the Liturgy*, p. 305.
9. *The United Methodist Book of Worship* (Nashville: The United Methodist Publishing House, 1992), p. 38.
10. *The Book of Common Prayer* (New York: Church Hymnal Corporation, 1979), pp. 363, 371.
11. *Book of Common Worship* (Louisville: Westminster/John Knox Press, 1993), pp. 71, 73.
12. Ibid., pp. 75-76.
13. Ibid., p. 145.
14. Philipp Melanchthon, *Apology of the Augsburg Confession*, in *The Book of Concord* trans. Theodore G. Tappert (Philadelphia: Fortress Press, 1959), pp. 255-56.
15. The Large Catechism, in *Book of Concord*, p. 454.
16. Trans. George MacDonald, in *Luther's Works*, vol. 53 (Philadelphia: Fortress Press, 1965), pp. 219, 253.
17. Brian Gerrish, *Grace and Gratitude: The Eucharistic Theology of John Calvin* (Minneapolis: Fortress Press, 1993). See also Pamela Ann Moeller, *Calvin's Doxology* (Allison Park, Pa: Pickwick Publications, 1997).
18. John Calvin, *Institutes of the Christian Religion*, ed. John T. McNeill, trans. Ford Lewis Battles, Library of Christian Classics 20-21 (Philadelphia: Westminster Press, 1960), p. 1445.
19. Ibid., p. 1414.
20. Ibid., p. 1422.
21. The Canons and Decrees of the Council of Trent, trans. J. Waterworth, in Philip Schaff, *Creeds of Christendom* (1877; reprint, Grand Rapids: Baker Book House, 1969), vol. 2, p. 179.
22. *A Directory for the Publique Worship of God* (Bramcote, Notts.: Grove Books, 1980), p. 22.
23. *Eucharistic Hymns*, hymn 57, p. 213.
24. *United Methodist Book of Worship*, pp. 54-80. One prayer, prepared by the Consultation on Church Union, is not included in this book.
25. *Book of Common Prayer*, pp. 333-43; 361-75.
26. *Lutheran Book of Worship* (Minneapolis: Augsburg Publishing House, 1978), pp. 109-13, and Minister's Desk Edition, pp. 221-26.
27. *Book of Common Worship*, pp. 69-73; 80-81 and 126-56; 165-400; 869-72; 929-32.
28. Apostolic Constitutions, in *Prayers of the Eucharist: Early and Reformed*, ed. R. C. D. Jasper and G. J. Cuming, 3rd ed. (New York: Pueblo Publishing, 1987), pp. 104-12.
29. Ulrich Zwingli, *Attack on the Canon of the Mass*, in *Prayers of the Eucharist*, pp. 184-86.
30. Odo Casel, *The Mystery of Christian Worship and Other Writings*, trans. I. T. Hale (Westminster, Md.: Newman Press, 1962).
31. *Baptism, Eucharist and Ministry* (Geneva: World Council of Churches, 1982), p. 10.
32. *United Methodist Book of Worship*, p. 36.

33. *Book of Common Prayer*, p. 370.
34. Ibid., p. 373.
35. *Lutheran Book of Worship*, p. 69.
36. *Book of Common Worship*, p. 69.
37. Irmgard Pahl, *Coena Domini I* (Freiburg: University Press, 1983), pp. 7-24.
38. *On the Lord's Supper*, in *Zwingli and Bullinger*, ed. and trans. G. W. Bromiley, Library of Christian Classics 24 (Philadelphia: Westminster Press, 1953), p. 235.
39. Conrad Grebel, "Letter to Thomas Müntzer," trans. Walter Rauschenbusch, in *Spiritual and Anabaptist Writers*, ed. George Hunston Williams, Library of Christian Classics 25 (Philadelphia: Westminster Press, 1957), pp. 76-77.
40. The Schleitheim Confession, in *Legacy of Michael Sattler*, ed. and trans. John Howard Yoder (Scottdale, Pa.: Herald Press, 1973), p. 37.
41. John Calvin, The Catechism of the Church of Geneva, in *Calvin: Theological Treatises*, trans. J. K. S. Reid, Library of Christian Classics 22 (Philadelphia: Westminster Press, 1954), p. 139.
42. *Eucharistic Hymns*, hymn 165, p. 248.
43. *Baptism, Eucharist and Ministry*, p. 14.
44. *United Methodist Book of Worship*, pp. 35, 38.
45. *Book of Common Prayer*, p. 372.
46. Ibid., p. 375.
47. *Lutheran Book of Worship*, Minister's Desk Edition, p. 259.
48. *Book of Common Worship*, p. 72.
49. Ibid., p. 141.
50. *Baptism, Eucharist and Ministry*, pp. 10-11.
51. *The Babylonian Captivity of the Church*, trans. A. T. W. Steinhäuser, Frederick C. Ahrens, and Abdel Ross Wentz, in *Luther's Works*, vol. 36 (Philadelphia: Muhlenberg Press, 1959), p. 35.
52. Calvin, *Institutes*, p. 1431.
53. *The First and Second Prayer Books of Edward VI* (London: Everyman's Library, 1964), pp. 222-23.
54. Daniel Brevint, "The Christian Sacrament and Sacrifice," in Rattenbury, *Eucharistic Hymns*, p. 187.
55. *Eucharistic Hymns*, hymn 116, p. 231.
56. Ibid., hymn 123, p. 234.
57. *United Methodist Book of Worship*, p. 38.
58. *Book of Common Prayer*, pp. 363, 375.
59. *Lutheran Book of Worship*, Minister's Desk Edition, p. 262.
60. *Book of Common Worship*, pp. 128, 71, 140.
61. The Apostolic Tradition, in Jasper and Cuming, *Prayers of the Eucharist*, p. 35.
62. *St. Cyril of Jerusalem's Lectures on the Christian Sacraments*, trans. R. W. Church (London: S.P.C.K., 1951), p. 74.
63. Liturgy of John Chrysostom, in Jasper and Cuming, *Prayers of the Eucharist*, p. 133.
64. *An Exposition of the Faith*, in *Zwingli and Bullinger*, p. 260.
65. Catechism of the Church of Geneva, in *Calvin: Theological Treatises*, p. 137.
66. Calvin, *Institutes*, p. 1405.
67. *Liturgies of the Western Church*, ed. Bard Thompson (1961; reprint, Minneapolis: Fortress Press, 1980), p. 209.
68. *First and Second Prayer Books*, p. 222.
69. *Eucharistic Hymns*, hymn 72, p. 217.
70. Ibid., hymn 16, p. 200.
71. Ibid., hymn 7, p. 197.
72. *Baptism, Eucharist and Ministry*, p. 13.
73. *United Methodist Book of Worship*, p. 38.
74. *Book of Common Prayer*, pp. 363, 369, 375.
75. *Lutheran Book of Worship*, pp. 111-12.
76. *Book of Common Worship*, pp. 72-148.
77. John H. McKenna, *Eucharist and Holy Spirit: The Eucharistic Epiclesis in Twentieth-Century Theology* (Great Wakering, Eng.: Mayhew-McCrimmon, 1975).

78. James F. White, *Christian Worship in North America: A Retrospective, 1955–1995* (Collegeville: Liturgical Press, 1997), pp. 175-81.

79. *United Methodist Book of Worship*, p. 39.

6. Commonly Called Sacraments

1. James F. White, *Sacraments as God's Self Giving* (Nashville: Abingdon Press, 1983), pp. 70-92.

2. James Dallen, *The Reconciling Community: The Rite of Penance* (New York: Pueblo Publishing Company, 1986), p. 158.

3. *The Sacrament of Penance*, trans. Theodore E. Bachmann, *Luther's Works*, vol. 35 (Philadelphia: Muhlenberg Press, 1960), p. 14.

4. *The Babylonian Captivity of the Church*, trans. A. T. W. Steinhäuser and Frederick C. Ahrens and Abdel Ross Wentz, in *Luther's Works*, vol. 36 (Philadelphia: Muhlenberg Press, 1959), pp. 81-82.

5. Ibid., p. 86.

6. Ibid., p. 88.

7. *How One Should Teach Common Folk to Shrive Themselves*, trans. Joseph Stump and Ulrich S. Leopold, in *Luther's Works*, vol. 53 (Philadelphia: Fortress Press, 1965), p. 121.

8. Beverley A. Nitschke, "The Third Sacrament? Confession and Forgiveness in the *Lutheran Book of Worship*" (unpublished Ph.D. dissertation, University of Notre Dame, 1988), chap. 1.

9. Thomas H. Schattauer, "Announcement, Confession, and Lord's Supper in the Pastoral-Liturgical Work of Wilhelm Loehe" (unpublished Ph.D. dissertation, University of Notre Dame, 1990).

10. The Schleitheim Confession, in *Legacy of Michael Sattler*, ed. and trans. John Howard Yoder (Scottdale, Pa.: Herald Press, 1973), pp. 36-37.

11. "Admonition on Church Discipline," ed. John C. Wenger, trans. Leonard Verduin, in *The Complete Writings of Menno Simons* (Scottdale, Pa.: Herald Press, 1956), p. 413.

12. Simons, "Account of Excommunication," in *Complete Writings*, p. 471.

13. Peter Riedeman, *Account of Our Religion, Doctrine, and Faith*, in *Anabaptism in Outline*, ed. Walter Klaassen (Scottdale, Pa.: Herald Press, 1981), p. 221.

14. Martin Bucer, Strassburg Liturgy, in *Liturgies of the Western Church*, ed. Bard Thompson (1961; reprint, Minneapolis: Fortress Press, 1980), pp. 168-69.

15. John Calvin, "The Form of Church Prayers," in *Liturgies of the Western Church*, p. 197.

16. *The Methodist Hymnal* (Nashville: Methodist Publishing House, 1939), p. 524.

17. "The Rules of the United Societies," in *John Wesley*, ed. Albert C. Outler (New York: Oxford University Press, 1964), p. 181.

18. *The House of Lords on Ritualism in the Church, Confession & Absolution: Shocking Disclosures* (Manchester: John Heywood, n.d.).

19. Richard Baxter, *The Reformed Pastor* (New York: American Tract Society, n.d.), pp. 156-59.

20. *The Book of Common Prayer* (New York: Church Hymnal Corporation, 1979), pp. 147-52.

21. *Lutheran Book of Worship* (Minneapolis: Augsburg Publishing House, 1978), p. 56.

22. *Book of Common Worship* (Louisville: Westminster/John Knox Press, 1993), pp. 1023-24.

23. Charles W. Gusmer, *And You Visited Me: Sacramental Ministry to the Sick and the Dying*, rev. ed. (New York: Pueblo Publishing Company, 1984), p. 32.

24. *Babylonian Captivity*, in *Luther's Works*, vol. 36, p. 118.

25. Ibid., p. 121.

26. Martin Luther, *D. Martin Luthers Werke: Briefwechsel*, vol. 11 (Weimar: Hermann Böhlaus Nachfolger, 1948), pp. 111-12.

27. John Calvin, *Institutes of the Christian Religion*, ed. John T. McNeill, trans. Ford Lewis Battles, Library of Christian Classics 20-21 (Philadelphia: Westminster Press, 1960), p. 1468.

28. Calvin, "De la Visitation des malades," in *Ioannis Calvini Opera Quae Supersunt Omnia* (Brunswick: C. A. Schwetschke and Sons, 1867), vol. 6, p. 108.

29. Ibid., vol. 17, p. 311.

30. *The First and Second Prayer Books of King Edward VI* (London: Everyman's Library, 1964), p. 261.
31. Ibid., p. 268.
32. *A Directory for the Publique Worship of God* (Bramcote, Notts.: Grove Books, 1980), p. 26.
33. Ibid., p. 28.
34. *John Wesley's Prayer Book* (Akron: OSL Publications, 1991), pp. 155-56.
35. *Book of Worship* [Church of the Brethren] (Elgin: Brethren Press, 1964), p. 230.
36. *The United Methodist Book of Worship* (Nashville: The United Methodist Publishing House, 1992), pp. 613-29.
37. *The Book of Occasional Services* (New York: Church Hymnal Corporation, 1979).
38. *Occasional Services* (Minneapolis: Augsburg Press, 1982).
39. *Services for Occasions of Pastoral Care* (Louisville: Westminster/John Knox Press, 1990).
40. *Book of Common Worship*, pp. 967-1022.
41. "The Order of Marriage for Common Pastors," trans. Paul Zeller Strodach and Ulrich S. Leupold, in *Luther's Works*, vol. 53, pp. 110-15.
42. *A Sermon on the Estate of Marriage*, trans. James Atkinson, in *Luther's Works*, vol. 44 (Philadelphia: Fortress Press, 1966), pp. 7-14.
43. Calvin, *Institutes*, p. 1481.
44. Bryan Spinks, "The Liturgical Origin and Theology of Calvin's Genevan Marriage Rite," *Ecclesia Orans* 3 (1986): 195-210.
45. "La Manière de celebrer le sainct mariage," in *Opera Omnia*, vol. 6, pp. 205-7.
46. *The Liturgical Portions of the Genevan Service Book*, ed. William D. Maxwell (Westminster: Faith Press, 1965), pp. 144-48.
47. *First and Second Prayer Books*, p. 252.
48. Ibid., p. 254.
49. Ibid., p. 258.
50. Mark Searle and Kenneth W. Stevenson, *Documents of the Marriage Liturgy* (Collegeville: Liturgical Press, 1992), p. 234.
51. *John Wesley's Prayer Book*, pp. 149-55.
52. Karen Westerfield Tucker, "Till Death Do Us Part: The Rites of Marriage and Burial Prepared by John Wesley and Their Development in the Methodist Episcopal Church 1784-1939" (unpublished Ph.D. dissertation, University of Notre Dame, 1992).
53. *United Methodist Book of Worship*, p. 122.
54. *Book of Common Worship*, p. 850.
55. Ibid., pp. 869-71.
56. Ibid., pp. 883-92.
57. *A Christian Celebration of Marriage: An Ecumenical Liturgy*, rev. ed., Consultation on Common Texts (Minneapolis: Augsburg Fortress, 1995).
58. Peter Lombard, *The Four Books of Sentences*, in *Peter Lombard and the Sacramental System*, trans. Elizabeth Frances Rogers (Merrick, N.Y.: Richwood Publishing Company, 1976), Distinction XXIV, xiv, p. 233.
59. Thomas Aquinas, "De Articulis fidei et ecclesiae sacramentis," in *Opuscula theologica*, vol. 1 (Turin: Marietti, 1954), p. 151.
60. *Babylonian Captivity*, in *Luther's Works*, vol. 36, pp. 106-7.
61. Ibid., p. 116.
62. Ralph F. Smith, *Luther, Ministry, and Ordination Rites in the Early Reformation Church* (New York: Peter Lang, 1995).
63. *The Ordination of Ministers of the Word*, trans. Paul Zeller Strodach and Ulrich S. Leupold, in *Luther's Works*, vol. 53, pp. 124-26.
64. Calvin, *Institutes*, p. 1476.
65. "Draft Ecclesiastical Ordinances, September & October 1541," in *Calvin: Theological Treatises*, trans. J. K. S. Reid, Library of Christian Classics 22 (Philadelphia: Westminster Press, 1954), pp. 58-59.
66. James Fredrick Holper, "Presbyteral Office and Ordination, American Presbyterianism: A Liturgical-Historical Study" (unpublished Ph.D. dissertation, University of Notre Dame, 1988).

67. Paul F. Bradshaw, *The Anglican Ordinal: Its History and Development from the Reformation to the Present Day* (London: S.P.C.K., 1971), p. 16.
68. *First and Second Prayer Books*, p. 311.
69. Ibid., pp. 292, 302.
70. Horton Davies, *The Worship of the American Puritans, 1629–1730* (New York: Peter Lang, 1990), pp. 213-28.
71. *John Wesley's Prayer Book*, p. i.
72. "On Sedilia and Altar Chairs," *The Ecclesiologist* 2 (1842): 91.
73. *Baptism, Eucharist and Ministry* (Geneva: World Council of Churches, 1982), p. 20.
74. Ibid., p. 22.
75. Ibid., p. 24.
76. *United Methodist Book of Worship*, pp. 667, 677, 705.
77. *Book of Common Prayer*, pp. 520-21, 533-34, 545.
78. *Occasional Services*, pp. 192-99. See also Paul R. Nelson, "Lutheran Ordination in North America: The 1982 Rite" (unpublished Ph.D. dissertation, University of Notre Dame, 1987).
79. Preface to the Burial Hymns, trans. Paul Zeller Strodach and Ulrich S. Leupold, in *Luther's Works*, vol. 53, p. 326.
80. *Liturgical Portions*, p. 161.
81. *A Directory for Publique Worship*, 28.
82. Westerfield Tucker, "Till Death Us Do Part," p. 233.
83. Susan J. White, *Christian Worship and Technological Change* (Nashville: Abingdon Press, 1994), pp. 72-80.
84. *United Methodist Book of Worship*, pp. 139-71.
85. *Book of Common Prayer*, pp. 469-507.
86. Ibid., p. 488.
87. *Lutheran Book of Worship*, pp. 206-14.
88. *Book of Common Worship*, pp. 911-46.

7. Future Prospects

1. Paul Tillich, *The Protestant Era*, trans. James Luther Adams (Chicago: University of Chicago Press, 1948), p. 112.
2. Ibid., pp. 94, 102-3.

GLOSSARY

Antipedobaptists groups opposing baptism of infants and small children, usually professing believers' baptism as preferable.

Aumbry a cupboard for holding the consecrated bread between celebrations of the eucharist.

Banns public announcement in church of intention to marry.

Baptism, Eucharist and Ministry an attempt to find ecumenical agreement on these three items, produced by the World Council of Churches in 1982 after many years of preparation.

Base communities small groups of Christians in developing countries, usually meeting without clerical leadership.

Believers' baptism baptism restricted to those of mature enough age to make their own public profession of faith.

Chrisom robes robes worn by newly baptized babies, sometimes used at their burial if they die young.

Concomitance the doctrine that the fullness of Christ is in every morsel of the consecrated bread and every drop of consecrated wine.

Council of Trent the chief agency of Roman Catholic reform in the Reformation period. It met intermittently from 1545 to 1563.

Daily office daily services of public prayer, required of those in religious communities and Roman Catholic clergy. Traditionally there were seven daily offices plus a night office.

Elements the bread and wine used in the eucharist.

Epiclesis a prayer of invocation for the Holy Spirit, especially in the eucharist. It may seek to bless the bread and wine or the community or both.

Gloria in excelsis a musical part of the eucharist, beginning with the words, "Glory be to God in the highest," sometimes called the Great Doxology in contrast to the *Gloria Patri.*

Host the bread consecrated in the eucharist.

Oblation an act of offering to God, specifically a part of the eucharistic prayer offering a memorial of Christ's works to the Father.

Opus operatum the concept that grace is caused and conferred automatically in the sacraments with the proper form, matter, and ministrant.

Pedobaptists those who practice the baptism of infants and small children as well as adults.

Pietism a movement in seventeenth- and eighteenth-century Germany and England that stressed informal inward devotion; often somewhat mystical and opposed to dry, formal, rigid orthodoxy.

Postils books of sermons, often published to help other preachers.

Preface an opening part of the eucharistic prayer. It often varies according to the season or occasion.

Pyx a hanging vessel, often in the shape of the dove, to contain bread previously consecrated at the eucharist.

Repristination the concept of returning to the practices of the New Testament church, often sought in nineteenth-century American frontier movements.

Reserved sacrament the consecrated bread remaining after the eucharist when kept for further communions or for the sick. It could be kept in an aumbry, pyx, sacrament house, or tabernacle.

Roodscreen a screen in medieval churches separating the nave (for the laity) from the chancel (for the clergy) and often with a cross (rood) over it.

Sacrament house a structure, usually of some height, inside a church to house the consecrated bread, usually for purposes of adoration.

Sanctus part of the eucharist prayer, usually sung: "Holy, holy, holy."

FOR FURTHER READING

Aulén, Gustaf. *Eucharist and Sacrifice*. Trans. Eric H. Wahlstrom. Philadelphia: Muhlenberg Press, 1958.

Barclay, Alexander. *The Protestant Doctrine of the Lord's Supper.* Glasgow: Jackson, Wylie & Co., 1927.

Barclay, William. *The Lord's Supper.* Nashville: Abingdon Press, 1967.

Barth, Markus. *Rediscovering the Lord's Supper: Communion with Israel, with Christ, and Among the Guests*. Atlanta: John Knox Press, 1988.

Brand, Eugene. *Baptism: A Pastoral Perspective*. Minneapolis: Augsburg Publishing House, 1975.

Brilioth, Yngve. *Eucharistic Faith and Practice: Evangelical and Catholic.* Trans. A. G. Hebert. London: S.P.C.K., 1953.

Bromiley, Geoffrey. *Children of Promise: The Case for Baptizing Infants.* Grand Rapids: Eerdmans, 1979.

———. *Sacramental Teaching and Practice in the Reformation Churches.* Grand Rapids: Eerdmans, 1957.

Brooks, Peter. *Thomas Cranmer's Doctrine of the Eucharist*. London: Macmillan, 1965.

Browning, Robert L. and Roy A. Reed. *The Sacraments in Religious Education and Liturgy*. Birmingham: Religious Education Press, 1985.

Cochrane, Arthur C. *Eating and Drinking with Jesus: An Ethical and Biblical Inquiry.* Philadelphia: Westminster Press, 1974.

Crockett, William R. *Eucharist: Symbol of Transformation.* New York: Pueblo Publishing Company, 1989.

Davies, Horton. *Bread of Life and Cup of Joy: Newer Ecumenical Perspectives on the Eucharist.* Grand Rapids: Eerdmans, 1993.

Duck, Ruth C. *Gender and the Name of God: The Trinitarian Baptismal Formula.* New York: Pilgrim Press, 1991.

Dugmore, C. W. *Eucharistic Doctrine in England from Hooker to Waterland.* London: S.P.C.K., 1942.

Eller, Vernard. *In Place of Sacraments: A Study of Baptism and the Lord's Supper.* Grand Rapids: Eerdmans, 1972.

Felton, Gayle Carlton. *This Gift of Water: The Practice and Theology of Baptism Among Methodists in America.* Nashville: Abingdon Press, 1992.

Fiedler, Ernest J. and R. Benjamin Garrison. *The Sacraments: an Experiment in Ecumenical Honesty.* Nashville: Abingdon Press, 1969.

Forsyth, P. T. *The Church and the Sacraments.* London: Independent Press, 1955.

Gerrish, B. A. *Grace and Gratitude: The Eucharistic Theology of John Calvin.* Minneapolis: Fortress Press, 1993.

Gilmore, A., editor. *Christian Baptism.* London: Lutterworth Press, 1959.

Heron, Alasdair I. *Table and Tradition.* Philadelphia: Westminster Press, 1983.

Jenson, Robert W. *Visible Words: The Interpretation and Practice of Christian Sacraments.* Minneapolis: Fortress Press, 1978.

Jones, Paul H. *Christ's Eucharistic Presence: A History of the Doctrine.* New York: Peter Lang, 1994.

Lehmann, H. T., ed. *Meaning and Practice of the Lord's Supper.* Philadelphia: Muhlenberg Press, 1961.

McDonnell, Kilian. *John Calvin, the Church, and the Eucharist.* Princeton: Princeton University Press, 1967.

Marty, Martin E. *The Lord's Supper.* Philadelphia: Fortress Press, 1980.

Moeller, Pamela Ann. *Calvin's Doxology.* Allison Park, Pa.: Pickwick Publications, 1997.

Oden, Thomas C. *Ministry Through Word and Sacrament.* New York: Crossroad, 1989.

Pittenger, Norman. *Life as Eucharist.* Grand Rapids: Eerdmans, 1973.

Pocknee, Cyril E. *Water and the Spirit: A Study in the Relation of Baptism and Confirmation.* London: Darton, Longman, and Todd, 1967.

Procter-Smith, Marjorie and Janet R. Walton, editors. *Women at Worship: Interpretations of North American Diversity*. Louisville: Westminster/John Knox Press, 1993.

Quick, Oliver Chase. *The Christian Sacraments*. London: Nisbet, 1948.

Reumann, John. *The Supper of the Lord: The New Testament, Ecumenical Dialogues, and Faith and Order on Eucharist*. Philadelphia: Fortress Press, 1985.

Saliers, Don E. *Worship as Theology: Foretaste of Glory Divine*. Nashville: Abingdon Press, 1994.

Schlink, Edmund. *The Doctrine of Baptism*. Trans. Herbert Bouman. Saint Louis: Concordia Press, 1972.

Sedgwick, Timothy F. *Sacramental Ethics: Paschal Identity and the Christian Life*. Philadelphia: Fortress Press, 1987.

Senn, Frank C. *Christian Liturgy: Catholic and Evangelical*. Minneapolis: Fortress Press, 1997.

———, ed. *Protestant Spiritual Traditions*. New York: Paulist Press, 1986.

Staples, Rob L. *Outward Sign and Inward Grace: The Place of Sacraments in Wesleyan Spirituality*. Kansas City, Mo.: Beacon Hill Press of Kansas City, 1991.

Stevenson, Kenneth. *Eucharist and Offering*. New York: Pueblo Publishing, 1986.

Stevick, Daniel B. *Baptismal Moments: Baptismal Meanings*. New York: Church Hymnal Corporation, 1987.

Stookey, Laurence Hull. *Baptism: Christ's Act in the Church*. Nashville: Abingdon Press, 1982.

———. *Eucharist: Christ's Feast with the Church*. Nashville: Abingdon Press, 1993.

Thurian, Max. *The Mystery of the Eucharist: An Ecumenical Approach*. Grand Rapids: Eerdmans, 1984.

Wainwright, Geoffrey. *Worship with One Accord: Where Liturgy and Ecumenism Embrace*. New York: Oxford University Press, 1997.

Wallace, Ronald S. *Calvin's Doctrine of the Word and Sacrament*. Edinburgh: Oliver and Boyd, 1953.

Watkins, Keith. *The Great Thanksgiving: The Eucharistic Norm of Christian Worship*. St. Louis: Chalice Press, 1995.

Weil, Louis. *Sacraments and Liturgy: The Outward Signs*. Oxford: Basil Blackwell, 1983.

World Council of Churches. *One Lord, One Baptism*. Minneapolis: Augsburg Press, 1961.

INDEX OF PERSONS

INDEX OF SUBJECTS